Teams Work!

A No-Nonsense Approach to Team Building

Joyce Mitchell

Woman's Missionary Union
Birmingham, Alabama

Woman's Missionary Union
P. O. Box 830010
Birmingham, AL 35283-0010

©2003 by Woman's Missionary Union
All rights reserved. First printing 2003
Printed in the United States of America
Woman's Missionary Union® and WMU® are registered trade-marks.

Dewey Decimal Classification: 302.3
SUBJECT HEADINGS: TEAM MANAGEMENT
                  LEADERSHIP—GROUP THEORY
                  GROUP RELATIONS TRAINING

Design by Janell E. Young
Cover design by Bruce Watford

ISBN: 1-56309-818-0
W033104•1203•2M1

To Andrea, Becky, Carol, Charles, Charlotte, David, Delores, the other Joyce, Linda, Lynn, Michael, Nancy, Reva, Sharon, Sylvia, Tania, and Wanda, who have been patient colearners in this teaming process.

Contents

Introduction

I recall vividly an adult learning experience I had while a student in seminary. The required class was called simply Group Dynamics. The professor was passionate about the subject. Each Tuesday evening for a couple of hours, a small group of men and women met to learn the basics of how individuals behave when they are placed in groups and given a task to perform. Our professor challenged us to do "silly things" (or so I thought at the time) like build a castle out of a paper bag full of odd supplies—newspapers, pasteboard mailing tubes, yarn, masking tape, chenille craft stems, etc. The only rule was that we accomplish this feat in total silence—no talking and no writing notes. The end result of my team's efforts was so lopsided few would have identified it as a castle. The valuable learning experience of the evening was the debriefing time during which we were able to talk and analyze our comical group miscommunication which led to the lopsided castle. Did we learn a few things about how adults behave and succeed or fail as a team? Yes.

After seminary graduation, I joined a church in Michigan where I was allowed to grow and try new leadership roles. In a church setting, I began to recall nuggets of what I had learned about group dynamics. I experimented and applied these tidbits on an unsuspecting group of church leaders called the church council. With good-natured tolerance, these volunteer leaders endured get-acquainted activities. They complied with my insistence on a written agenda. They were willing to articulate a written mission statement. They even adhered to time frames for discussion. As we met together, they affirmed that we seemed able to do our work more efficiently. We were doing church council in a new way. I learned the truths and wisdom about teams were also relevant in the junior high school where I taught, in community organizations, and later in the denominational organizations where I served.

Most recently, Woman's Missionary Union, where I have served for nearly 20 years, implemented a major shift from traditional departments with a hierarchical, supervisory chain to a team-based culture. This change was one of "seismic proportion," declared one senior executive. The company, in its 114th year of existence, had never before so thoroughly moved people around, physically and in the way they were asked to work. The experience has been a treasure trove of new learnings each day about what team means. My observations and involvement with teams has intensified as I try to simultaneously facilitate team training, analyze teams which appear to be floundering, lead a couple of teams, and model a new paradigm of team leadership.

Since those early seminary days—now nearly 30 years ago—I've never built another castle. Professionally, at church, and in my community, I have been a member of groups charged with accomplishing complex and significant tasks, as well as simple and straightforward tasks. I have led teams. I have walked away from most team experiences with a new appreciation for the great potential of teams. Even the teams that failed provided insights about what not to do next time.

Personally and professionally, I have grown increasingly convinced that teams are an energizing and amazing way to accomplish the purpose of an organization. Teams work! I am a proponent of learning and teaching the skills that are critical for the development of team participation.

There are scores of books on the subject of teams. I've read many of these books and will steer you to several I have found helpful. The focus of this book is a small message: teams work. There are approaches I have learned as a team practitioner that will help anyone who finds herself working with one team or many. Practice makes a team leader. I have tried to include some theory as well as some real world experience. Not all my team experiences have been successes, and I suspect the reader may identify with that. I have not tried to create an abstract treatise on organizational development, although those books do exist. Nor am I providing a sophisticated psychological model of team dynamics. You must find that elsewhere.

I have discovered that when my mind is in the team mode (i.e., when I am thinking about the dynamics which may apply or boost the success of one of my teams), learnings jump out at me from a variety of places: movies, billboards, advertisements on TV, the sports page of the newspaper, etc. A co-worker calls this the "red car principle." She likens the process to someone who wants to buy a red car. A person has in her mind that she is going to buy a red car. In shopping junkets to car dealerships, she only notices red cars. Blue cars or green cars never make it onto her radar. After a red car is purchased, the owner still notices red cars. When the idea of team is fully ingrained in your mind, ideas related to team, team concepts, and team analogies jump out at you from the unlikeliest places. The things that make a team click are never externally imposed: the team members jump into the experience and learn from each other. Success as a team breeds success. The team is more ready to attempt loftier goals after it has experienced small successes.

This book is an effort to unpack and highlight the practical things I have learned on the topic of working with teams in a church and in the workplace. I hope individual readers who are also leading teams or serving on teams will find this productive material. Happy team reading!

When Two or More Gather

"A team is a group of people committed to a common purpose who choose to cooperate in order to achieve exceptional results."[1]

Inside Team: *My earliest bona fide team experience occurred in elementary school when Mrs. P. divided the whole class into random work groups of five or six students. Boys and girls were on the same teams. She set the stage for our learning adventure by describing what teams did and the nature of teamwork. Each group received an assignment which required creative thinking, planning, research, and a communication plan. Class time each day was dedicated for the teams to meet and work on the project. At the end of the month, each team was required to make a presentation to the class. The team would receive one grade based on their collective efforts.*

I do not remember what letter grade my group received. I do recall several lessons which grew out of that initial teamwork experience, including (1) several classmates treated the group assignment as a joke; (2) it's better to establish a leader at the beginning rather than in the middle of a team process; (3) a few team members (the girls) did most of the work when others on the team (the boys) refused to be serious; (4) not everyone valued "getting an A"; (5) we had much room to improve in our skills as team players; and (6) our teacher noted the end result (class presentation) of our teaming was as varied as the teamwork (process) she observed among the groups.

A team is a team is a team . . .

I like to collect words. It's a cheap hobby since words are free and they appear everywhere! Think about the many choices you have when you are searching for a term to describe two or more people. You could say

Group, work group, team, cluster, family, bunch, wad, section, department, division, circle, organization, club, collection, congregation, aggregate, class, gang, company, league, crew, choir, ensemble, quartet, trio, clique, crowd, set, knot, clan, etc.

Because I have been an active church member over a long period of time, I know many large groups exist within the church. With self-deprecating humor, we often make light of the sheer number of committees, and meetings, it takes to keep the church going. Some of the groups are formal (committees elected by the church). Others are informal: the regular "lunch bunch" that gathers following Sunday morning worship.

Church is not the only arena in which groups or teams abound. The workplace has taken to the organizational structure of teams. Both nonprofit and for-profit corporations are among the practitioners of teamwork and team structure. Teams thrive in public and private schools. A social phenomenon, which has mushroomed in popularity, is the book group or reading club. Individuals from the workplace, the neighborhood, or even casual acquaintances meet to read and discuss a book which they have selected in advance. Opportunities for team involvement are everywhere!

Activity versus task groups

On the continuum of groups from formal to informal, it is easy to see some groups are engaged in activity. The activity is appealing and meets the need of its members. Churches may have dozens of activity groups: prayer groups, prayer-walking groups, study groups, service groups, ministry groups, fun groups, discussion groups, support groups, evangelism groups, fellowship groups, visitation groups, etc. Members voluntarily participate in the group. Christian education groups (or Sunday School classes) often begin with the new school year. At the end of the school year, joining a different group is frequently an option.

Activity groups flourish in the community and through the workplace. Often these groups are bound together by a common interest: the local gardening club, the Tuesday evening bowling league, or the monthly Scrabble® club.

Another typical category of group is the task group. They may be called committees, councils, leadership groups, boards, etc. People are generally enlisted, elected, or appointed to serve on task groups. Theoretically, task groups focus on a specific purpose. They have a mandate. For example, the church is without a pastor. A pastoral nominating committee is elected. Their task: find a pastor to present to the congregation. The group comes into existence, they meet, and at the end of a certain period of time they either accomplish their task, or they fail to accomplish it. If they succeed, the church welcomes a new pastor. If the group fails, usually a new committee is elected.

One distinction between an activity group and a task group is the outcome. A prayer group prays. If the members of a prayer group gathered each week for a month, and no praying occurred, then I suspect the group would fall by the wayside. Their reason for existence is to pray. The group members learn by engaging in this activity. They grow. They never completely master prayer, but they learn by doing.

It is not necessary to classify each type of team or group with which we are involved. But it is significant to have a level of awareness concerning the dynamics of a group of people who meet together. And it is productive to understand the contribution or difference an individual member or leader can make to the success of the team's outcome.

The focus of this book is the team which undertakes a task: a task team. Narrow in scope, these groups have a specific, timebound purpose for existence: to select furnishings for the new educational building, to provide oversight for the church finances and budget, to plan and implement the Christmas bazaar, etc. When the furnishings are installed, or the bazaar is over, the team ceases to exist. The task has been accomplished. The team celebrates its accomplishment and is grateful for the newfound free time which once had been filled with team meetings.

No task, no team

Task groups have been a feature of church culture since the very first committee. Appointing a committee is a time-honored and effective way a church accomplishes its mission. In recent years, the term *team* has become interchangeable with *group* or *committee*. Churches may have a transition team, a worship team, a leadership team, etc. These task teams share the distinction of having a specific purpose; possess both a leader and members; and are subject to the dynamics which are typical among groups in the business world, in politics, in the community, and wherever else teams emerge.

Within many churches a collection of committees called standing committees may also exist. Members of these committees face the challenge of identifying the specific task of the committee. One I was once elected to required involvement of ten persons from the congregation. It met monthly. A church staff member met with the committee, though the official leader of the committee was a laywoman. After four months of meetings, the committee had done little except hear a report from the staff member each month and engage in some general discussion about the education program in the church. Members who had been eager to be a part of the committee began to find excuses to be absent. Were these committee members slackers or unwilling to be committed?

Upon reflection, I think the reality is a group of sincere men and women had said yes initially to the opportunity to help shape the educational program of the church. After meeting for several months, it became apparent the norm for this committee was to hear reports, engage in discussion, and provide little strategic direction or decision making about the program. The leader was perpetuating what had always been done on that particular committee. Those who served never wrestled with a compelling task or vision. Failure to identify a meaningful task resulted in growing disinterest on the part of those who were members.

Standing committees, particularly, would benefit from a periodic examination of why the committee exists. Analysis or discussion in the early weeks of a new committee's life of why they are meeting gives new and old members an opportunity to shape the possible direction of even a mundane standing committee.

Teams are not mysterious

A writing teacher once critiqued my prose as having a high "fog index." (He didn't appreciate how often I resorted to a thesaurus to replace simple, clear words with their multisyllabic sisters!) This book is an effort to reduce the fog index about teams and the team process. After all, teams are a staple of the way we do church and organizational life. We spend an inordinate amount of time, personally and professionally, "in meetings." You may be the leader as well as a member of multiple teams. In addition to accomplishing the team purpose, wouldn't you be gratified to have had a positive experience with the team process?

All teams share a number of Big Picture elements in common, including people, purpose, culture (or atmosphere), a time frame, and a meeting plan. As we take a long look at a typical team, it may be insightful to look more closely at each of these elements.

People

Think back to the last time you were waiting in line to purchase a ticket to a movie. Those people who lined up with you reflect a team in one narrow respect: you do have a common purpose. The similarity ends once you have secured your ticket. You scatter to a variety of theaters to view different feature movies. The constituency on teams may seem as random as the people in line at the movies . . . at first. The fascinating thing about teams is the process of being involved together to accomplish a task enables diverse people to know each other more deeply. The skills, competencies, experiences, and personality foibles of each individual are revealed as you meet to pursue the task your team has.

Experience has revealed the more diversity which exists on a team, the greater potential the team has to be strong, effective, and successful at accomplishing its task. Diversity on a team simply means team members are different. The differences which make for strong teams might include gender, ethnicity, work experience, value systems, perspective, personality, generation, etc.

When confronted with the challenge of selecting a pastoral nominating committee, my church intentionally nominated both longtime church members as well as newcomers to the congregation, both men and women, and members who had retired as well as one who was still in high school. After functioning for nine months and enduring countless hours of meetings, this diverse seven-member committee was able to present a unanimous recommendation to a grateful congregation. Their diversity was a plus in finding a candidate which delighted the congregation.

From my formative experience with teamwork in the fifth grade, I am mindful that team members always have the right to choose to participate on teams. Even Mrs. P.'s role as an authority figure did not convince some of the members on my team that they should participate. They joked, they played, they distracted; but they never bought into the task which our team was given. Adults on teams are not too different. They choose to be full-fledged team participants. As Pat MacMillan observes, "Cooperation is a choice made by each individual team member. This decision is based on his or her perception of whether or not cooperation is the best way to achieve a desired goal. Therefore, teams are 'volunteer' organizations."[2]

In the workplace setting, in spite of the fact individuals are actually paid to serve on teams, the volunteer model still holds true. An organizational chart may place Sam on a team, but Sam alone decides whether he will participate fully on the team. He can attend meetings, make an occasional contribution to the discussion, but is he sold out to the purpose for which the team was formed? Only Sam makes that decision. Team members do not have to overtly sabotage the team in order to be nonparticipants. They can simply demonstrate a low level of energy or passion for what the team is about. They resist making their best contributions or investing themselves in the process. Teams are volunteer organizations.

How many people should be enlisted to serve on a team? According to team experts whom I have read, a range of between five and ten team members is a practical, working number. Trying to coordinate schedules for more than ten individuals can be a nightmare in logistics. Fewer than five might not bring the necessary skill sets to the task. There is no perfect number for a team constituency.

Inside Team: *WMU launched its new structure with approximately 20 teams. The smallest team represents a single function (human resources) and has only 2 individual members. The largest team also represents a single function (graphic design) and has 13 team members. Most team members serve on a "home" team and at least one other team in a support role. Great care was given to physically move team members to workspaces which adjoined their fellow team members. I was skeptical about the necessity to move team members into proximity to each other. Looking back, I see teams have expressed their individualistic personalities because they are close enough to pop into and out of each others' work stations. A couple of teams have instituted novel team rituals like TAPP (Thursday Afternoon Popcorn Parties). Held in the common area outside their work cubicles each Thursday afternoon at 2:00, multiple teams gather for a brief popcorn break together.*

Purpose

The key factor for a team's success is a clear, compelling purpose. A purpose statement simply answers the question, Why does this team exist? Generally, purpose statements evolve in a couple of different ways. Team members can brainstorm and supply their answers to the purpose question. There can be a lively exchange of ideas and philosophy about what the team's true purpose is. Ultimately, the purpose statement should be reduced to a sentence or two which has meaning for the team. It is also possible a mandate or charge of purpose might be handed to the team by management or a company's board of directors. In either case, purpose statements need to reflect the thinking of the members of the team, and be owned by the team itself.

I've already alluded to a common pitfall among standing committees: unclear purpose. If a team has been in existence for months or even years, it is likely the membership has changed. It is always valuable to revisit the purpose for which a team was once created. The current members of a team can update and refresh the language of a team's purpose statement. Even if the team's purpose exists in the formal written language of the church bylaws, the team may consider the KJV statement of their purpose. What do they perceive their team purpose is in *Contemporary English Version* or the *Living Bible* paraphrase?

Task teams have a distinct advantage as far as purpose is concerned. The pastoral nominating committee knew exactly what work they were elected to perform: find a senior pastor for the church. They certainly had latitude about how they did their task, but ultimately success for their team was their recommendation of a pastor who would be acceptable to the community of faith.

Oversight committees and standing committees have more of a challenge. Their question might well be How will we know we are successful as a committee? A discussion of this question early in the team's time together will allow all team members to voice their expectations and vision for the success of the team.

When is a team not a team? A true team is distinguished by the sense of shared vision which they have. Many groups of people are merely work groups. I think the important thing is not to labor over "Are we a real team or not?" A group who keeps focusing on what needs to happen, in terms of results, will evolve into a team. A team which is a true team will be known by its fruits.

Inside Team: *When the 117 WMU staff members were transitioning from departments to teams, many of the teams invested a high level of energy in creating their original purpose statements. Hours were spent crafting sentences, editing, revisiting, and refining the words. Looking back, I suspect we were somewhat obsessed with the purpose statements, trying to dis-*

cover the perfect combination of words. There are no perfect purpose statements, only statements which reflect where the team members are at the beginning of their journey together. Since then, nearly all of the teams have tweaked and modified their original statements. Team composition has changed as staff members have left and new staff members have joined the teams. A team recognizes the purpose statement for what it is: words to set their direction.

Culture

Each team has a unique atmosphere or spirit. This is particularly noticeable when the membership of the team remains intact over a period of time. The variables which shape a team culture include the personalities of the team members. The unique chemistry or blending of individuals can create memorable team experiences. Some teams are formal in their culture; others are informal. I don't remember talking specifically about team culture with a team; but looking back on dozens of experiences, differences in culture are quickly discerned. There is openness in the culture of some teams. Others take a while to get warmed up. The culture of one team might welcome new members. The spirit of another team might be very businesslike and efficient, seldom straying from its task.

At the earliest meeting of a team, a savvy team leader will often lead the members in a discussion concerning team expectations. Such a discussion will result in creating a series of operating rules or norms by which the team members agree to live by. These rules are valuable as the team matures and wades into the complexities of its task.

One team which I led was charged with a significant task of weathering the transition between the retirement of one pastor and the arrival of a new pastor. At our very first meeting, the team members agreed upon the need for the ability to be completely candid in our discussions about congregational history, needs, challenges, etc. While we did not label this norm as "straight talk," I have since come to recognize it as such. A second norm we wholeheartedly affirmed was we would not talk about our team task, even with each other, outside of the team meetings. We placed a premium on confidentiality. And as the team met for nearly a year and wrestled with difficult issues, that operating principle served us well.

The codes of behavior, operating principles, or norms are an insightful window into the culture of a particular team.

Inside Team: *Teams often cultivate and express a distinctive spirit. The WMU team which is responsible for publishing preschool products has a unique challenge in that one of their team is a telecommuting team member. They have conquered geography by using technology to stay in touch. They also embody a genuine culture of celebration as their team accomplishes its goals. In fact, one of their operating principles is related to celebrating the accomplishments of the team. When a recent music CD for preschoolers sold 1,000 copies, with tongue in cheek, they declared it had "gone platinum," and celebrated accordingly.*

Time frame

Often a team is launched with a specific mandate or charge. Accompanying this charge is a statement or the implication of the amount of time which the team will have to deliver its result. An event planning team would naturally be expected to conclude their work in time for the event to be conducted. Other teams are given a charge with an open ended time frame. The pastoral nominating committee was not given a specific deadline for delivering their result, but the implied message from the congregation was, "Our pastor has retired. We want another leader for the congregation as soon as the team process will allow. We trust you to do your work."

Particularly with teams which do not have a specific date by which their work is to be complete, ongoing communication in the form of updates with the congregation is a good working principle.

An initial discussion by the team, preferably held early on, should examine the scope of what they're trying to accomplish and their projected time frame.

Even a team that has a complex task needs the accountability of knowing the congregation expects a result by a particular date.

Inside Team: *On the last day of September, our employees were part of functional departments. On the first day of October, those same employees were configured into a variety of teams. How does time frame relate to the transition which these employees experienced? Part of the team orientation each team experienced was coming together to express its purpose and to begin to articulate goals which would enable the team to accomplish its purpose. A characteristic of a good goal is the date by which the goal will be accomplished.*

Meeting plan

Meetings are the norm for adults in the workplace and in congregational life. Not all meetings are equal, however. It is far simpler to announce, "We need to have a meeting," and even get it on the calendar than to execute the actions which ensure the meeting is productive and successful. A meeting plan is a series of steps. There are things that need to occur before, during, and after a meeting.

From the simple task of selecting a time and place to meet, to the development of an agenda, to the preparation which must be done before the meeting, to the facilitating of what occurs during the meeting, to the follow-up after the meeting; each of these actions could fall under the umbrella of meeting plan.

Particularly at the beginning of a team's history, the person who is the leader of the team bears the responsibility for the meeting plan. As the team matures, often team members step up to implement various steps of the meeting plan. The effectiveness of the leader in terms of administrative skills is key to the success of the team. The leader is aware of the pace of what a team is accomplishing during the meetings and what needs to be accomplished in order to succeed at their intended purpose.

Inside Team: *Staff members in my organization are accustomed to meetings. With the introduction of the team culture, meetings became even more significant because meetings are the playing field for teams. Individuals on each team had individual accountabilities (such as editing a magazine or performing accounting functions). When the team meets, however, the team meets to make progress on the team purpose. Many of the teams included in their operating guidelines that an agenda, distributed in advance of the meeting, was an expectation for their team.*

Stages of team growth

Many books which deal with team dynamics describe four predictable stages of team life. The terminology may vary, but the stages include forming, storming, norming, and performing. Each stage reflects a developmental task through which the team must grow.

When a team first forms, there is a level of uncertainty about many aspects of the team process, if not the task. Some of the team members may be relative strangers to each other. Questions will surface and must be dealt with: Why do we exist? What is my role? What are the rules which will guide us as a team? To whom are we accountable? What are the expectations of others for our team? When do we have to deliver our team's end result? How shall we get at our task? This is clearly the forming stage. And all teams wrestle with these questions.

A savvy team leader helps surface the questions and enables the team members to contribute their input to pose answers to the questions.

The forming stage leads seamlessly into the storming stage. Because team members are diverse individuals, conflict is a naturally emerging by-product of being in the same room together. The leader's ability to keep the team focused on their purpose and to facilitate openness in hearing from all team members will enable the team to weather the storming stage.

The norming stage occurs as team members grasp how they can collectively perform the task of the team. Each one recognizes and respects the roles of other team members. Working styles are identified and processes emerge. Meetings become times of productive collaboration with the team making strides toward accomplishing their purpose. Team members rely on the pronoun *we* rather than *I* as their collective identity strengthens.

The final stage of performing is an appropriate term for a mature, well-functioning team. There is cohesiveness and a synergy which did not exist in the early stage of forming. This team is capable of initiative and creativity because they have tapped into the "collective IQ" of the team.

Inside Team: *You are the leader of a team of six co-workers who have been selected to plan and implement your company's booth at a regional trade show. You have thorough information about budget and logistics of the upcoming show. Your company has participated in this annual show for the past 15 years and is committed to participate this year. Each year's* effort has been a "dog-and-pony" show which has surpassed the previous year's effort in terms of elaborate, expensive, labor-intensive work.

At the initial team meeting, it is clear several team members are openly skeptical about the effectiveness of this show. You hear statements like, "I already have plenty of work on my plate" and "I can't believe we're going to spend $_____ on this one show."

As the designated team leader, what are your options? What would you do in this initial meeting? What would you do next?

Team Leader Technique: *If you are leading a new team, it is likely some people on the team may have reservations about the team experience. They may be doubtful about the potential success of collaborating with each other, reluctant to make a change, uncertain about their roles in the new structure, etc. As team leader, give the team an opportunity to voice those concerns by using a mind dumpster. Place a small wastepaper basket or other receptacle in the middle of the room. Provide half sheets of paper for everyone. Invite members to think about the worst thing that could happen because this team has formed. What is a personal fear or concern you have about working with each other? Encourage the team to fill up as many half sheets as they like and after a few minutes (three to four) wad the papers up and sail them into the wastepaper basket. Assure the team it's normal to have negative thoughts about new ventures. After the symbolic tossing of doubts, fears, etc., the team may be more ready to envision what they can do as a team.*

One Person: Leader

"Leadership in today's world requires far more than a large stock of gunboats and a hard fist at the conference table."[1]

Inside Team: *Seven employees of Daffodil Baskets, Inc., were charged to explore the possibilities of outsourcing the information technology service for their company. Their company's core business was the production of baskets. The team members knew each other, though they represented different functional areas including design, customer service, marketing, and production. The CEO appointed one staff member, B., as leader of the team and asked the team to bring a recommendation.*

B. arranged for the logistics of the first meeting, including refreshments, and reminded the team of their task. No one questioned what the team was to do. In fact, several team members immediately offered strong opinions about why the outsourcing would be the only sensible direction. As the discussion unfolded, the voices of two team members became more and more of a dialogue, pressing toward outsourcing. B. made a few attempts to focus the discussion on more than a single solution, but the two talkers continued to push their point.

After two frustrating hours, the meeting was over. Several team members gathered their papers with

apologetic shrugs saying they had "another meeting."
Two team members had said virtually nothing. B. was
frustrated because the talkers had monopolized the
agenda. The team did not have a recommendation
which they could endorse collaboratively, nor had they
identified the pros and cons of outsourcing. They also
failed to surface what the next step would be. B.'s final
words were "We may have to meet again."

What went wrong? Was it a simple failure in lead-
ership?

Not all team leaders are created equal

Team leaders can be categorized dozens of different way.
On the simplest level, a leader is successful or not successful. Leaders are effective or they're lousy. Books on leadership often label individual types of team leaders based on
positive or negative traits. While labels can precisely
describe a leader (to the point and even amusing), a single
label hardly encompasses the complexities of any team
leader.

Team leaders are, above all, human beings who are in
the midst of growing, changing, and evolving in terms of
who they are.

To honor the multidimensional nature of team leaders,
it is good to view team leaders through multiple lenses.
Three such lenses are (1) characteristics of a leader, (2)
what team leader characteristics look like in action, and
(3) the team leader's balancing act.

1. Characteristics of a leader

Is there one personality trait or style which is a key to success for a team leader? Probably not. Among the scores of
assessment tools and instruments which enable one to gain

insight into unique personality characteristics, often the results place people on a continuum in categories such as:

- Introverts and extroverts
- Those who possess a good self-image and those who lack self-esteem
- Those who are self-confident and those who are not
- "People persons" and solitary people
- Those who are conscientious and those who are not
- Those who are aggressive and those who are more passive
- Those who display their emotional nature and those who give little weight to their feelings and are more logical
- Big Picture folks and those who focus on the minute details
- Those who are risk takers and those who are adverse to risks
- Persons who are concrete, here-and-now types of individuals and persons who think more futuristically and in terms of "what if?"
- Servant leaders versus the CEO-type of leaders

Effective team leaders may emerge from any one of these categories, regardless of where they find themselves on the continuum. The team leader's success is more dependent upon whether the membership of the team provides a counterbalance and responds to the leader's personality.

Beyond personality, the team leader brings a variety of strengths to the table. These might be viewed in terms of core competencies. What are the potential skill sets which will lead to effectiveness in leading a team? Here are a few:

1. Interpersonal skills
2. Planning/Organizing
3. Conflict management

4. Presenting
5. Teamwork
6. Written communication
7. Decision making
8. Goal orientation
9. Leadership
10. Flexibility

Interpersonal skills enable a leader to get along with a variety of diverse team members. A good team leader is engaged and interested in the team members. Communicating effectively is a key skill here. A leader who listens to team members and seeks to understand their viewpoints is greatly valued. Treating team members with respect and striving to understand their attitudes and perspectives is essential as well. A. is a team leader who excels in making members of her teams feel valued. It is easy to observe how this plays out by watching her with her team: she makes eye contact with any member with whom she's communicating. Even her posture as she listens indicates she's interested in what the team member is saying. Her interest in each member has a ring of authenticity. She makes the team meetings pleasant by using her humor and playfulness as the team task is tackled. Discussion flows freely between team members because they sense their input is valued.

Planning and organizing have the ring of boring tasks which are done only if the team is compelled to do so. Those whose work is dependent upon the team fulfilling its task appreciate a team leader who honors whatever time frame the team has been given. A team leader who is an engineer by vocation used the logical and practical skills he had mastered in his profession to lead a team in his church to create a new organizational structure. His willingness to let the team roam far and wide in early meetings to explore many possible scenarios encouraged creative thought. After several meetings, he noticed the team had diverged (i.e., been all over the map). Now it was time to converge (i.e., settle on a possible structure). At each meeting he came armed with grids and data which reflected what the team had talked about at their last meeting, and what a structure would look like if those ideas were implemented. He obviously had done much assimilating of what the team had previously discussed. The task was complex, but the thorough planning and organizing skills of the team leader enabled the team to bring a successful proposal to the congregation.

Conflict management is an essential skill for leading teams which are diverse. Team leaders recognize the differences of opinion concerning the team task do not have to damage relationships. In fact, conflict is a good sign the team members are thinking and care enough about the task to put on the table an alternative solution. The leader's role becomes one of diffusing the tension which accompanies ideas which are poles apart. Team members who are in adversarial positions can become emotional. Early in my professional life, a supervisor made an observation about how I led teams: "When Joyce cares deeply about something, her voice inflection rises, and she speaks quickly." The essence of her message to me was "chill out." Take a breath. Regroup. Try and hear what a team member who has a different opinion has to say. I learned to be alert to my tendency toward defensiveness, particularly when I felt strong ownership of a viewpoint.

Presenting is a basic communication skill. At times the team task may be straightforward and the path to accomplishing it is apparent to everyone involved. Other teams have been down the path before, and one can look at the steps which led to their success and do what they did. Other team tasks are multilayered and complex. The team leader at the very outset must organize the information to be presented in succinct and logical sequence. A church team I once led had a three-page mandate which outlined what we were to accomplish, the issues which might impinge upon our task, how we were to relate to the congregation as we did our work, and a timeline for delivering the result. Fortunately the timeline was months into the future. An initial challenge was to assimilate the lengthy mandate and present clear and understandable information to an earnest group of church members who wanted our team to succeed.

William Barclay, a great biblical commentator, described himself as never having had an original idea in his life. Yet he felt he had explained and expounded other men's ideas very well.[2] A team leader who masters the art of assimilating the contributions of team members, their ideas, and brilliant thoughts will ensure the success of the team.

Teamwork involves a cultural shift, particularly for those of us who have learned to value individualism, or who have been a part of departments or groups in which we have been simply told what to do. The team leader's role is one of calling forth the best efforts of each team member. The team purpose provides the organizing principle which allows each team member to make his or her best contribution. The staffs in many congregations now function as a team, with the senior pastor leading the team. George Cladis writes, "The most effective churches today are the ones that are developing team-based leadership."[3] The team purpose? The mission of the church. Unleashing the collective IQ occurs when team members collectively become more than any one of them can be individually. *Synergy* is a term used to describe a team which utilizes teamwork. It is evident that a group of individuals who are becoming a team make their team mission priority. They take off their individual hats when they meet together, and their success or failure is an outcome which they shoulder collectively.

Written communication is a matter of deciding what message needs to be delivered and then crafting it with clarity for whatever audience will receive it. Organizing information in logical sequence aids the reader in grasping the point or coming to a natural conclusion. One team of 7 charged with planning and conducting a national meeting for a large audience held daylong meetings in which much creative discussion was generated. The multipaged documents which were generated following the meetings often were a verbatim record of who said what in the meeting. When the next meeting occurred, the team developed the habit of rehashing issues which had been discussed, and even decided, in a previous session. Often new creative ideas were added to the original idea. One practical role of a team leader is to assimilate whatever has been noted in official minutes and make visible to the team what it has created/decided/agreed to previously. If the team affirms the direction, then new territory can be explored.

Decision making is one of the processes universal to teams. It is also a process which can make a team a pleasurable, productive experience or a dreaded nightmare. There are numerous ways for a group of people to make a decision. A healthy practice that promotes good teamship is the team talking about decision making before they start down the road to having to make decisions. Consensus decision making, a path chosen by many groups, involves everyone voicing their opinions. Discussions are often lively. The team leader or designated facilitator guides the team in sorting through the implications of each possible solution. Then the team agrees on a course of action. Does consensus mean 100 percent of the team is in agreement with the decision? If you've talked about what consensus means (in advance), it may be that your team has agreed it's OK for consensus to represent the best decision which the team can agree to and commit to in the time frame you have. If you've defined consensus as 100 percent agreement, then be prepared for lengthier meetings to allow the fullest discussion and creation of solutions which are totally acceptable to everyone. A bit of wise advice from many who are experienced with teams is if you can avoid putting a team decision to a vote, you avoid polarizing the members into those who want "green paint" and those who want "lavender paint" for the walls.

The goal orientation of a team leader grows out of the skill which the leader has to keep her eye on the ball. A team is formed. A purpose is either handed to the team or established by the team. What happens next? The team establishes goals which will enable the team to accomplish its purpose. At each team meeting, the team leader enables the team to focus on taking steps toward accomplishing its goals. What actions have to occur before the goal is achieved? Which team member is the best person to be the champion of a specific action? A team leader with little goal orientation could allow team meetings to evolve into general discussion times. Focusing on the goal and establishing a pace for the team meetings, which includes an element of urgency that the team stay focused on the goal, is up to the team leaders. When I polled a team I once led with a "How am I doing?" kind of question, several of the team members responded they felt driven by my adherence to the agenda and accomplishing exactly what was outlined for the meeting. Their input influenced my behavior. I relaxed a bit about strictly completing every item on the agenda. There is a balance which the leader needs to exhibit: creating adequate time for discussion and buy-in by all the team members.

The value of leadership, theories, models and styles of leadership, and the necessity for genuine leadership is discussed at length in books related to both business and the church. A team leader must demonstrate leadership to the team, if the team is to succeed. I suspect B.'s lack of success with her Daffodil Baskets, Inc., team was due to her inability to regain control of her team meeting. A team leader may possess varying degrees of each of the ten characteristics which I have described. The team leader may possess unique competencies which I have not mentioned. Among the many leaders with whom I have served, I have appreciated the leader most who demonstrated a spirit of optimism and the positive expectation that our team could do what we had been charged to do. Someone once described the leadership of Helen Fling, a former national president of my organization, as "Women would follow Mrs. Fling if she led them to walk straight up a brick wall. No questions asked." That's leadership.

Flexibility is a prerequisite for team leaders by virtue of the fact they work with people, and not all people think like I do. The frequently heard lament that change is the only constant we have today demands a team leader be agile in adapting to change. When the membership of a team changes, the team essentially is a new team. The team leader's role? Enable whatever momentum which has built up to continue, while helping the new member make a contribution to the team task. Flexibility enables a team to be productive in the midst of transition and even chaos. The team leader for whom flexibility is a habit seems to know exactly when it's time to shift gears with the team. The team leader should model that flexibility. As a member of a team in a previous profession, management kept adding to our team task. At each meeting the team leader would inform us of another element or issue which we needed to address. Some of the team members, without the presence of such an able team leader, would have been negative about the additional tasks. The team leader has such a winsome leadership style that she gracefully and with good humor led our team to respond to the unexpected demands of an expanding task. She modeled flexibility for us.

2. What team leader characteristics look like in action

Team scenario:	Action of team leader:
The XYZ Team consisted of men and women from several departments within the company. The culture of one department was laid back, while another was best described as formal.	At the first team meeting, the team leader led the members to write down a series of operating principles, or norms, which would guide their team meetings. These norms addressed both behavioral issues ("We will listen to each other") and procedural issues ("We will begin and end on time").
The XYZ Team identified a series of challenging goals which would lead their team to be successful at accomplishing their purpose. Each goal was subdivided into actions which team members would have to implement, and a date by which the action was to be completed. Team members had multiple actions for which he or she was responsible.	The team leader's name appeared as the responsible person beside a number of appropriate actions. A team leader does real work, in addition to facilitating the meetings.
In early meetings of the team, when the team members were getting to know each other, discussions often halted at a point when the issue was complex or information was unclear. A team member might look to the team leader and openly inquire, "What should we do now?"	The team leader was quick to respond, "I'm not sure. Do any of you have an idea about a next step?" A team leader does not have all the answers. Often, she is able to point to a possible resource person or a path for getting an answer. But, just as likely, when the team collectively analyzes their options, a team member has the answer to the question, What should we do now?

Team scenario:	Action of team leader:
Taking team minutes can be a task which no one eagerly volunteers to do. This was the case with the XYZ Team. One after another team members made excuses about their handwriting, their lack of computer, etc. Yet, having a record of what the team discussed, decisions, etc., was important.	The team leader quickly announced she was willing to take notes at the team meetings. She even commented (and seemed sincere in doing so) that jotting down main points of their discussion helped her think and keep on track with the team deliberations. This team leader demonstrated servant leadership for her team.
The task of a particular church team required meetings at least every two weeks. The team members, all volunteers, were waning in their enthusiasm for the task. At nearly every meeting, one or more members were absent, at times without letting the team leader know.	The team leader continued to call meetings because of the urgency of their team's task. She maintained an optimistic and energetic spirit in the team meetings, and team members who did attend felt the sessions were productive. She was consistent in her commitment as a team leader and did not allow the meetings to deteriorate into a whining session about members who were absent.
The church council which had appointed a team expected frequent updates on the team's progress. They requested both written and oral reports.	Initially, the team leader made the oral reports about the team's progress. As the team developed, the team leader, who had been willing to be visible, delegated the oral report role to the team's most able public speaker. She continued to ensure the written reports were circulated to the church council.

Team scenario:	Action of team leader:
A cross-functional publishing company team was engaged in strategic planning. The major challenge which the team faced was how to market the books which they produced for specialty audiences.	The team leader communicated in advance with the marketing team member that she would be the team facilitator during the meeting. The team leader was flexible in passing the baton (or marker) to the functional expert.

3. The team leader's balancing act

A good team leader has a finely tuned sense of balance, for there are a variety of issues which she must balance, not the least of which is the task which the team has been given and the process by which they address the task. Is one more important than the other? Probably not. The team would have no reason to exist unless it had a purpose or task. On the other hand, unless the team meets and is productive in working on accomplishing their purpose, the purpose lies dormant.

Task

Inside Team: *When a company which had operated with functional departments made the transformation into a team-based culture, staff was exposed to a variety of learning and training experiences. As over 20 teams held their initial meetings, they were challenged to create a purpose statement for their team. Staff members agonized over exactly which words were the best words or right words to reflect their purpose. They approached the process as a chore, and for some it was an intense labor. They were framing a meaningful series of words which answered the question, Why does your team exist? So much emphasis was given to the purpose that one team leader observed teams becoming obsessive about their statements. Lively discussion and parsing of words ensued. Team leaders would poll each other and compare statements. Finally, an outside trainer took pity on the team leaders and revealed that while purpose statements are important (they drive the team!), they are not permanently chiseled in marble. The team creates the purpose statement; and the team, upon further reflection and growth as a team, can make changes to it, refine it, and even create new versions of it.*

After the teams had been meeting for a year, it was interesting to watch the ease with which they looked at their team purpose statements, felt a sense of ownership over them, and were not afraid to change them.

Process

Not every person who is asked to lead a team is a skilled facilitator. Perhaps that leader's skills rest more in the administration area. And yet, whatever happens during the meeting will either lead the team toward productivity, or be considered, at worst, a waste of time. During team meetings, the team has an opportunity to work on its task. And the team leader role is to coach the best contribution from each team member. If facilitating a team meeting is a skill which the leader has not mastered, a wise leader would look toward delegating the facilitation to another person on the team.

Leading the team you're dealt

Another significant balancing activity is developing a team out of a group of people which, very likely, you did not handpick. In an ideal world, a team leader would be allowed to select each person who serves on her team. She would use criteria which fit the task and surely end up with a compatible group of people who would carry out the purpose with style and efficiency. Many teams are like arranged marriages: you get whoever the deciding body (your parents) chooses for you. How does a team leader work with a group which she did not choose? Perhaps this is the ultimate test of team leader flexibility. If, however, the people who comprise the team seem to be missing a key skill or competency, the team leader does have the responsibility to involve, if possible, a resource person who would bring that skill to the table. On a team I led recently, the challenge was to bring a proposal about how my company could "manage its knowledge." Bright and creative people made the contributions of which they were capable; but it was not until I recognized an information technology person was the missing component that the team began to make some progress.

Inside Team: *In one team experience within my company three individuals actually share the role of team leader. The team is charged with a function which is broad: leadership development. Each of the team leaders have an element of the leadership task for which they are individually responsible, but as the team comes together goals are established for what the team can accomplish collaboratively. Each team leader assumes a primary role for leadership for a quarter of the calendar year. When the next quarter roles around, the leadership shifts. Administrative and facilitative functions are thus rotated. Shared leadership of a team can succeed when the team leaders identify how they will approach the task.*

Team Leader Technique: *With any team you're leading, check the team pulse at regular intervals to see how you are doing as a leader. On a half sheet of paper, print these three open-ended statements: What would you like me to stop doing? What would you like me to keep on doing? What would you like me to start doing? Invite team members to jot down any response they have. No names are necessary. Just candor. Use this input to shape the way you lead the team.*

Everyone
Is a Team
Member

"If dialogue and problem-solving exchanges are dominated by those at the top of the formal hierarchy, the opportunity for each member to contribute in different ways is severely hampered."[1]

Inside Team: *Hollyhock Baptist Church is a young church with a history of short-tenured pastors. No pastor had ever reached retirement in its pulpit. Several sought other congregations after wearying of conflict within the congregation. Pastor Paul seemed to be headed toward becoming the exception to the forced termination pattern which Hollyhock Baptist Church had cultivated.*

Pastor Paul, a mature man of faith, with several congregational experiences on his résumé, observed, "You people seem to have an issue with pastoral authority."

The staff members who worked closely with Pastor Paul noted he exercised a firm grip on all decisions related to the church. One staffer described the pastor as "large and in charge." The staff talked about his controlling leadership style to members of the congregation and, inevitably, Pastor Paul was encouraged by the personnel committee to consider retirement. He did.

Hollyhock's interim pastor was of a different genera-
tion and leadership style than Pastor Paul. From the
beginning of his interim, Pastor Sam conveyed the
message to the church staff, "I consider us a team."
The ministerial team now discussed decisions which
had been strictly pastoral domain under Pastor Paul.
Individuals were involved in carrying out various visi-
ble roles which previously had been the pastor's role.
The staff team blossomed. Their sense of being valued
as contributors to the church's mission was enhanced.
Pastor Sam enjoyed the experience as interim as
much as the congregation. The committee charged
with finding a new pastor determined a key criterion
they would look for in their next leader was an indi-
vidual who was at ease with a team-based ministerial
approach. They found one.

Even in a traditional church structure team-based
leadership can work!

No cookie cutter team members

The only things team members may appear to have in common is they breathe, and they bear the label of team member. From this point on, comparisons break down. Team
members are as highly individualistic as thumbprints or
snowflakes. Their minds engage differently. They seldom
speak, or listen, the same. Some express their ideas clearly
and succinctly. Others struggle with putting their ideas
into words. Some say virtually nothing during the entire
meeting, while others are nonstop talkers. You may have
team members who are perennially sunny in their tem-
perament and full of positive energy. As you become familiar with another individual, you steel yourself for a
naysayer's remarks or can't-do attitude. You have learned
to rely on some team members to relieve the stress of a
tense moment with levity. Others you learn will try to lead
the group to "chase rabbits," or to explore a topic far afield

from your team purpose. You may have a team member who sits on the fence about issues, seeming to see both sides. Another team member, concerned with expedience, pushes the group to make a decision, any decision. Team members may be heavily invested in the purpose of the team and express this interest with passion and a sense of urgency. Other team members appear neutral, noncommittal, or even lackadaisical about the team's work.

While it is easy to assign a team member to a particular box, it is also likely the individual may choose to change boxes. For example, when a team member chases rabbits, it may be the team hasn't clearly zeroed in on what they are trying to accomplish as a team. As soon as the team purpose crystallizes and is unavoidably clear, the tendency to chase rabbits, or philosophize about a variety of subjects, may wane.

The wonder of teams is that they are able to accomplish anything!

Because team members represent a variety of personalities, background experiences, cultural viewpoints, education, communication styles, skills, etc., perhaps a more profitable approach for looking at members as a whole is to reflect upon what their team roles are in relationship to the purpose of the team.

Formal roles

Broadly speaking, there are formal and informal roles among team members. Usually, someone has been assigned to be the team leader. If not, then an early order of business for the team is to choose a team leader. Team leader is one formal role. Other team members may be asked to fill the roles of facilitator (although often the team leader assumes this role), recorder, etc. One team frequently compiled information in graphs or charts and needed the formal role of visual designer on their team. A timekeeper may be an appropriate person on a team which must have strict adherence to the time frame of discussion items on an agenda. Another team valued their refreshment break and created the role of snack person for their meetings. One team lightheartedly created a "goaltender" role for a member to keep the team on target with progress on team goals. The team may also choose to rotate the formal roles among team members.

Often, an individual has been enlisted to serve on a team because of a skill or expertise which she has. As a teenager, I was asked to serve on my church's administrative council to represent the viewpoint of youth in our congregation. It is frequently instructive for everyone on the team to hear what unique experience or skill a person brings to the team task. The team leader can facilitate such a sharing of information in the early stages of team development by asking, "Why do you think you were asked to serve on this team?" There may be some jaded members who respond, "Because I have a pulse and said yes." This is also a good opportunity for the team leader to affirm what the individual team member might bring to the team.

One team member, self-deprecating about her skills for the team task, was affirmed by a fellow team member, "But you're so faithful to attend the meetings!" Attendance is a necessity for team success.

Informal roles

Informal roles are fluid. Every team has a multitude of informal roles which enable the team to make progress toward their purpose. It may be someone else on the team excels in the role that is usually yours. Consider these typical informal roles which any team member can play and can often be passed between team members:

- Actively listens to the discussion of a team and then sums up the gist of the discussion for the benefit of the whole team.

- Voices a far-out, creative idea which would ultimately stretch the team.
- Affirms the good input from fellow team members.
- Adds clarification to the idea or information which another team member has expressed.
- Asks provocative questions which lead to deeper understanding.
- Mediates between two opposing points of view.
- Enumerates specific implications should the team take a certain course of action.
- Relieves the tension by making a humorous remark.
- Pays attention to those team members who are quiet and reserved and opens the door for them to contribute ("What do you think, Mary?").
- Articulates what seems to be the next step for the team to take.
- Volunteers to complete some work outside the team meeting which will enhance the team purpose.

Five influential factors

Numerous factors can affect the give-and-take between team members and ultimately have an impact on both the formal and informal roles which team members assume. Among many factors these five are particularly notable in coloring and shaping the team dynamic.

• **Gender:** Ideally, a team would be composed of both men and women members. The diversity of the male and female viewpoint would thus be represented. Often, one gender or the other prevails. In my workplace of 21 different teams, women lead 19 and men lead 2. On the teams themselves, there are usually more women than men. When one gender prevails, team dynamics can be affected.

A basic and critical process which affects the success of a team is communication. Skilled observers of communication agree that men and women communicate differently. One communication consultant boils down verbal cues between men and women to several distinct differences.[2] Men frequently assume the superior role in conversations. This is evident in the longer utterances of men, the fact that they speak directly, and that they may interrupt. Women may assume the subordinate role in conversations (speaking in shorter utterances, adding adjectives, adverbs, disclaimers, and tag questions) and allow interruptions by stopping their talking.

Harral describes other qualitative differences of speech between men and women. Men may order or command, make statements, and get right to the point. Women pose requests, ask questions, and often apologize or give thanks during their conversations. Though these observations apply in general, certainly individual men and women may choose to act differently.

• **Generation or stage of life:** Where are team members in terms of their generation? Much has been written about the impact of an individual's generation (i.e., different values and cultural icons) on who they are and how they live their lives.

If your team members are an eclectic combination of Matures (born before 1945), baby boomers (1946–64), Generation X (1960–80), and Millennial (1981–94), what a learning opportunity will unfold for your team!

It is risky to pigeonhole any generation. But imagine for a moment one team with a Mature who may espouse traditional values such as dedication, sacrifice, hard work, and conformity; alongside a baby boomer who values optimism, teamwork, personal growth, and health and wellness; joined by a Generation Xer who voices a cynicism about work, business, and career; and a Millennial who may bring to the table strong technological savvy, a respect for honesty (and the willingness to be frank), a love for feedback, visuals, and fun.

Each generation possesses unique characteristics. There are no rights and wrongs, just generational differences based on shared experiences.

• **Position:** In relationship to a workplace team, position refers to a person's job in the company. A team member, who happens to be the CFO, may be deferred to by teammates on every financial issue. In truth, he or she does bring unique financial information or perspective. However, it is the team as a whole who tries to make the decision, solve the problem, etc. Others on the team may also have experience with financial issues, and the position of the CFO alone should not give his or her opinion extra clout.

An individual who is a creative type, such as a graphic designer, may find herself the arbiter of any question or matter related to design or creativity. Actually, all team members are capable of weighing in on creative matters, brainstorming on a creative level, etc.

Often team members who want to defer to an individual because of his or her position tax the skills of a team leader. You can see the church ministerial staff has particularly tricky waters to navigate in order to be accepted as team members when sitting alongside church members. Staff must strive to be team members and not necessarily the voice of the expert because they are paid church staff.

In non-workplace teams, one's career position often colors the way that team member is treated by other team members. Team members who are educators by profession find others expecting them to speak for all who teach. Those who are nurses are the voice of all health professionals. Stay-at-home moms represent the broader category of all women who are not currently pursuing a career. Too, the fact a team member belongs to a particular ethnic or racial group may influence the team to expect that person to speak for all African Americans, etc.

• **Education:** Team members who have a variety of educational credentials can pose a challenge for establishing equality or level ground among the team members. Establishing an environment in which each member can put forth his or her best thinking is the ideal in a team situation. Advanced degrees, diplomas, or certifications may or may not enable a team member to be a valuable team participant. The team is, after all, pursuing a task. It is the task or the purpose which gives the team members a reason to be sitting in a meeting together, working on advancing toward the purpose.

A wise team leader is attentive to the impact which the educational levels of team members have on others who are on the team by paying attention to the subtleties of communication. If one or more members have accomplished a doctoral level of education, and offhand remarks are made, or the tendency to defer to the educated is noticed, the leader can implement an intervention.

The lack of formal education may be a sensitive issue with some team members. If vibrations of insecurity or self-deprecating humor seem to emanate from a team member, the team leader can shed the light on what gifts and skills each team member brings to the task, and value that individual who does not have the formal degrees. There's a reason or purpose for everyone on the team.

• **Thinking style:** It is no surprise that adults think differently. Yet it is common that each of us believes others probably think like we do. When confronted with a situation in which differences of opinion are expressed, some team members will shake their heads in bewilderment that anyone could think other than the way they do.

There are scores of tools, assessments, and inventories which can give team members insight into the way they think. Some are complex and need to be administered by a trained leader. Others are simple. Some tools involve a cost. All tools will likely provide some value as the team comes to grips with how each of them thinks differently. An appreciation for something as simple as whether the team member likes to process information internally (i.e., reflect on what's being said) or externally (i.e., say aloud what he or she is thinking even as he or she thinks) can influence the dynamics of a team.

If the team is a newly formed one, the team leader may choose to help the team members get to know each other by having the whole team experience a thinking style assessment together. One helpful tool is found in Bobbi DePorter's book *Quantum Learning*. By reading sets of words and selecting the ones which fit the team member, the individual learns whether he or she is a concrete sequential thinker, a concrete random thinker, an abstract random thinker, or an abstract sequential thinker. The instrument is self-scoring and can prompt a lively discussion based on the individual's preferred thinking style.[3]

Consider these typical team members: Lois needs to organize tasks into step-by-step processes and strives for perfection. John has a highly experimental attitude and sees things from many different points of view. Ben is a reflector and often seems to be very much into his own world and detached from the group. Shelly is great at analyzing information and zooming in on what's important, key points, and significant information. And who are these four individuals? Members of your team, each representing a very different thinking style.

Your team purpose may be to design a product, plan an event, plot a strategy for the future, or select the color of paint to be used in a remodeling effort; but you can see that Lois, John, Ben, and Shelly are going to make different contributions. That's part of the beauty of teams!

On-boarding: adding to the team

Ongoing teams lose team members from time to time, and on occasion add a new team member. How does the team assimilate a new individual? Someone has coined the phrase *on-boarding* to describe what happens when a new person joins a team.

Anyone on the team can lead out in welcoming the new team member. The leader, in particular, will ensure that the newcomer is aware of what the team's purpose is, an overview of the team's culture, how they operate, roles, etc. Often a newcomer is successfully integrated when the team leader (or some other designated individual) provides an orientation to the team's work. This activity is most helpful when done in advance of the first meeting. The new team member knows what to expect, a little about the culture of the team, how to participate, etc. Too, the rest of the team has a moment to formally welcome the new member and begin to see the kind of contribution he or she can bring to the team.

The team dynamic changes when someone new joins the team. While it is not practical, efficient, or even possible to totally begin again as a team, a review of the team purpose, the operating guidelines, and where the team perceives itself in terms of its goals and progress toward its task is a good review for current members. And, the "refreshing" provides an excellent way for the new kid on the block to begin to become familiar with the ebb and flow of this team and the way it operates.

Inside Team: *I felt slightly overwhelmed when I was elected to serve on a board of trustees for a community hospital system. This was my first venture onto a health-care board. I recall the practical help provided by the chief officer of the division who invited me to his office for lunch. He tailored a one-on-one orientation. Over several hours, he familiarized me with the vision, strategic plan, budget, and other information which enabled me to feel more aware of the new arena of teamwork I was entering. The following 9 years of service in this role were years of learning and possibly some contribution as well because a responsible leader had helped me to come on board.*

Once upon a time, there was a team . . .

As a child, I enjoyed stories beginning with "Once upon a time." Even as an adult, I gravitate toward stories or movies that have a linear plot line. The writer moves the action forward in a neat, orderly, chronological fashion. First one thing happens, then another, finally another, etc. Fiction books or movies that jump around in the way the story unfolds or the point of view are not my favorites.

Most teams begin in a once-upon-a-time fashion. Individuals are brought together. They have a purpose to explore and customize. At the outset, several elements of team dynamics begin to emerge. These variables affect the members of the team. While everyone on the team is aware of the existence of these factors, no one team member or even the leader controls them. The factors are the two critical and dynamic processes which all teams experience: communication and relationships. The trickiest thing about both communication and relationships is that they occur simultaneously, each spinning in a path of its own. The complexity of team dynamics is clearest when a team looks at the way it communicates and the state of its relationships.

Teams have had lofty successes and floundered based on their skills in both communication and relationships. An awareness of the importance of these factors can enable a team to overcome barriers which affect team performance.

Communication

Well-accepted interpersonal communication data remind us that only 7 percent of our communication is the words we say. The other 93 percent is nonverbal. And how do we nonverbally communicate? Thirty-eight percent is involved in the tone and inflection of our voice. And 55 percent is found in the facial expression and posture we use while we're talking.[4]

In chapter 5, I will describe team operating principles in greater depth. It is vital for a team to think about, and try to put into words in advance of beginning to work on their purpose, what constitutes acceptable communication in team interaction.

Within my company's 21 teams, a majority of the teams expressed operating guidelines which were suspiciously similar, including:

- We will use straight talk.
- Silence means agreement.
- We will listen to and respect each other's ideas and opinions.
- We will not interrupt each other.
- We will attack the idea, not the person.
- We will talk about team business with each other, not to outsiders.
- We will discuss divisive issues face-to-face.
- We will be open with each other.

Part of the similarity was undoubtedly the influence of the team trainer who stressed to the team leaders the importance of identifying the parameters or boundaries of communication before we tried to function as a team.

Inside Team: *Virginia is a team leader who does a lot of talking in her team meetings. The team members occasionally share their observations, being careful not to challenge her opinions directly. Following the team meeting, the members gather privately to discuss how the team could be a better team if Virginia understood how she contributed to the problems. Virginia, meanwhile, confides in her assistant that she wonders if the team will ever be effective if they continue to be yes-people in the meetings. No one ever discusses in the full group the concerns aired after the meetings.*

Would you suggest a path of action for Virginia?
For one of the team members?

Relationships

The interactions among team members over a period of time constitute the relationships which team members have with each other. It may be a relief to know it is not necessary for individuals who share a team alliance to be best friends. They do not have to regularly socialize with each other, have adjoining offices, or share similar functional responsibilities. There are several strands which, when woven together, serve to support strong team relationships. Those who lead, participate, and observe team behavior note the characteristics which lead to strong relationships on a team: acceptance, trust, respect, courtesy, understanding, and mutual accountability.[5]

How do the strands, or characteristics, play out in a team meeting?

• **Acceptance:** Though each team member represents a different functional role, all members are affirmed and valued as equal participants. Some of the team members are salaried workers; others are hourly workers. One team member is the leader. Several of the team members have a long work history with the company; others have just joined the staff. Some of the team members are recognized as creative. Others are known as wordsmiths or financially minded. All have an equal opportunity to speak, to propose an idea, to voice a solution, to disagree with the rest of the team, etc. The team leader is vigilant and careful to include all in the discussions which make up the team meeting. If the more talkative members of the team are sidelining one member, the leader injects an observation or opens the door for the shyer team member to register an opinion. The team IQ is enhanced when all of the members are encouraged and enabled to participate to the maximum.

- **Trust:** A key tool for establishing trust among the team members is the covenant, or set of operating guidelines, which the team establishes at the very beginning of its being. Trust is deepened and developed as each team member is able to observe that all members are abiding by the principles which the team set forth. If the operating principle is that the meetings start on time, then whoever is facilitating begins the meeting on time even if the team leader has been delayed by a phone call, etc.

- **Understanding:** Getting to know each other is a key activity for individuals who have not worked on a team together before. Simple get-acquainted activities can enhance the ability of team members to feel a level of understanding for diverse viewpoints. When conflict crops up, and it will if all team members participate, a crucial activity is the ability of a proponent of each viewpoint to be able to voice the opposing viewpoint. Clarifications can occur as those with polar opposite viewpoints strive to put the opposing opinion in their own words.

- **Respect:** At times a challenging exercise for team members is to merely listen to the viewpoints of those who approach a decision or try to solve a problem using a different set of assumptions. Respect plays out in the team meeting by the fact that team members are paying attention while everyone speaks and are not resorting to eye-rolling or other body language cues which indicate they don't take seriously the opinion being stated.

- **Courtesy:** Very akin to respect is the simple act of courtesy. Team members may have to feign this characteristic, but its absence speaks volumes. One team member found it impossible to express a clear message in a simple brief format. Her style was to ramble on, digress, and start and stop her train of thought. Ultimately, she expressed an opinion, and often the opinion was based on a significant and novel thought. The team members, however, had to exercise great courtesy because it took her a while to get to her destination.

• **Mutual accountability:** Good relationships on a team can rise or fall on the willingness of team members to deliver what they say they will do. For the eager beaver team member who quickly volunteers to fulfill a task and at the next meeting has not produced or researched what he or she promised, the relationships on the team will be strained. Good communication on a team demands that someone voice the disappointment or obstacle this team member has created by failing to follow through. An effective team will hold each other accountable to their commitments, thus enabling a team to succeed.

Team Leader Technique: *Give the team opportunities to evaluate how they are doing as a team by closing a meeting with these two open-ended questions: What are we doing well? What could we do better? The input can be informal and jotted on a flip chart, or you can ask the team members to respond on paper and collect the results.*

A Purpose Drives the Team

4

"Regardless of whether the life of the team is temporary or long lasting, its purpose is the motivation for its existence."[1]

Inside Team: *Since it's beginning, the congregation called Twin Pines Church valued Christian education for both children and adults. The church employed a full-time staff member who gave direction to the program. It also had a 12-member committee of laity known as the Education Committee. The group met each month and was chaired by a lay member. The staff minister served the committee as a resource person.*

Nancy was excited about being elected to serve on the Education Committee. A junior high teacher, she had some ideas which she was eager to explore with the committee. Others who served on the committee were experienced in teaching in the church.

At the initial meeting of the Education Committee for the new year, the lay chairman welcomed the new members, led in prayer, and distributed the agenda. The chairman turned to the staff person to interpret attendance reports, position vacancies, budget report, and directions for the future. An upcoming event on the calendar was discussed, and the team members gave input into how to encourage attendance and communicate the event in the community.

By the end of the meeting, Nancy's excitement had dimmed slightly. Because she was a newcomer, she anticipated the "next month" would give her an opportunity to raise some of the issues and ideas she had for strengthening the church's education program.

The next month's meeting was almost identical to the first meeting. As was the next meeting and the next. Halfway through the year, Nancy began to sense this committee was not a place in which her time was being well spent. She stopped attending the monthly meetings. Her absence was not followed up on other than a note in the committee minutes.

What went wrong? Was she simply a poor match for the task? Were her expectations out of sync with the team purpose? Was the team in a rut? Was there poor leadership at the top? Did the ministerial staff have too much influence?

The sketchy scenario does not give all the pertinent details, but one fact is clear by its omission: There was no orientation for new members, nor was the team as a whole, with new members at the table, reintroduced to the team purpose. It's likely that at one point in its history a task, charter, mission, or purpose was spelled out for the team. What was the wording? And how would this new set of team members interpret and envision the implementation of the task?

What is a purpose?

A purpose is simply a series of words, strung together, which tells why the team exists.

The Adult Resource Team exists "to inspire and equip adults to influence the world for Christ."[2]

A few guidelines to keep in mind while drafting a purpose statement:

- Keep it brief (a page-long document has too much content to enable the team to remain focused on what they're trying to do).
- It can be broad and directional (however, the goals which grow out of it will be specific, have time frames, etc.).
- A purpose statement can be achievable within the upcoming year (and when the purpose is achieved, the ongoing team has the joy of creating their next purpose).
- Use outcome-based language (what do you want to see happen as the result of your team being together?).
- Try not to obsess about writing a purpose statement (if you've spent several hours, that is probably sufficient).
- Don't compare your team's purpose statement with another team's. Creating purpose is not a contest.
- Check the purpose pulse of your team from time to time by asking, "Is this still relevant for us?"

Once the purpose statement is created, the team can envision a future in which its purpose has become a reality. For example, the Adult Resource Team imagined a world in which adults would

- be able to share their faith,
- have a global vision for their lives,
- see ministry and evangelism as interrelated,
- "think" WMU as the source of missions resources,
- see prayer as a vital part of missions,
- be actively involved in ministry,
- be able to express why they exist in relationship to missions,
- know their place in missions.

Who creates the team purpose, anyway?

Ultimately, the team creates its own purpose. This is true even if a purpose statement is presented to the team. The tributaries which feed into team purpose vary according to the nature of the team.

Nancy's committee, for example, is an ongoing group. A look back in the committee minutes, official documents, or church bylaws would reveal why the church established an education committee to begin with. Many ongoing committees, teams, and work groups operate off of a purpose statement which was officially adopted when their team was first established.

Does this mean its purpose is permanently etched in concrete? Possibly, depending upon where the verbiage resides and the implications or difficulty of revising the statement. However, the unique opportunity, which all teams have, is to look deeply at even the oldest, most long-standing statement of purpose. The team examines whatever words exist from their collective perspective as a team. The team thus interprets what the purpose means in the day in which they live. They imagine ways in which they will carry out the purpose.

Each team is unique. A team has never gathered together in quite its current composition, with these particularly gifted individuals, poised to offer their skills and time. Even an archaic, weary purpose which weighs like an anchor on an ongoing team can be revisited and mined for meaning. The team has latitude, even a responsibility, to strategize about how the purpose will be carried out today. How can new energy and excitement be injected into the work of a team, work group, or committee which has a long history?

Purpose statements are totally team territory to customize and personalize. Ideally, the team owns the purpose. The more the team disassembles and reassembles the purpose statement, the more they make the purpose theirs. Through the engagement of discussion, team members begin to internalize the purpose in ways which are impossible to predict. Chalk it up to the mystery of the synergy which characterizes teams.

I led a transition team in my church several years ago. We had a mandate from a small group within the church. I was excited about leading the team, thrilled with the individuals who had agreed to serve, but a little confused by the two-page purpose statement which was handed to us as a map. Realizing everyone on the team needed to hear any interpretation, I asked our team-to-be to meet once with the entity that called us into being. The meeting lasted several hours. Everyone attended. Good dialogue ensued. And our team, charged with a sensitive but significant task, got off on the right foot with our purpose. We had heard it from the horses' mouths, so to speak, and sought clarification while we were all seated around the table together. A clear purpose served as the glue which held our team together through the nine months of our service.

A unique circumstance exists among groups, usually in a workplace, who transition from traditional, functional departments into teams. Previously, they operated in a comfort zone with a supervisor who made final judgment calls, and even told them what to do. Now, thanks to management's fascination with the idea of teamwork, overnight they have become the XYZ Team.

In some instances, management gives the team, in writing, a charge, or statement of mission. They outline what they expect from this group who are now functioning as a team. Management does not always include specifics, but provides broad parameters for the team. Those parameters grow out of the mission or the vision of the company.

The bottom line is the purpose is the boss of the team. The purpose drives the team. The purpose provides fuel for the engine which is the team.

Inside Team: *Such was the case in the 115-year old publishing entity for which I work. The restructure within WMU was a radical and thorough restructure. One 35-year veteran staff member described the restructuring changes as the most pervasive in her entire career with the company. Management was seeking to change the very culture of the organization, not merely shuffle people around in terms of office space and titles.*

What did the new team environment look like? Staff members found themselves clustered around functions (mail room, information technology, customer relations, etc.) or audience teams (adults, students, children, etc.). The immediate challenge each team faced was to put their heads together, tap into their collective IQ, and write a purpose statement.

Looking back at our early efforts, I am amused with how much effort and sweat we expended in trying to craft perfectly worded purpose statements as if some ideal statement existed. Small teams of two or three members, and teams of ten or more members seemed equally obsessed by the purpose-crafting exercise. Given our history as a publishing entity, coupled with the fact that many employees are overachieving women, this should not have been a surprise.

A wise team coach suggests a newly formed team engage in a discussion about their purpose at their first meeting. Capturing thoughts and themes on a white board is often helpful to spark ideas from everyone on the team. Notes are taken on the ideas generated in the session. Then one or two team members are given the task of writing the purpose statement. They may not deliver the final version because the team should always have the latitude of the last word on their purpose statement The efforts of an individual wordsmith or even two will move the team along efficiently toward the purpose. The team bears the responsibility for determining how relevant their purpose statement is. It is the team's prerogative to revisit it and make changes when the team feels change is desired.

A temporary team wrestles with purpose

Another type of team purpose is one which guides a short-term team. This team is pulled together to address a specific need. The need is expressed in a straightforward manner, may be very detailed in terms of what is expected, and usually specifies a time frame. Like my transition team experience, the team receives its mandate from a third party. A purpose may be written in terms of what the team is expected to do, such as:

- to find and recommend a new staff member;
- to plan an event such as an anniversary celebration for the organization;
- to propose solutions to a problem which the organization has;
- to envision or dream a future for the entity and the actions it will take to get there;
- to analyze options for a major expenditure and bring a recommendation;
- to develop and implement a communication campaign to promote the organization to the rest of the world;
- to dream up a new product or service which meets the needs of a certain audience.

When the team produces an acceptable result, the team is disbanded. Its work is done. Does such a team need to rewrite the purpose statement at the outset? Not usually. But, the team does have to understand the boundaries of what they are being asked to do. The initial purpose discussion is focused on how we should approach our task.

Are there multiple possibilities of approach? What are the givens for the task? What do we know or what do we need to know in order to do our work? Are there models within our organization for this kind of task? How are we expected to communicate our progress to whatever entity has brought us into existence, and who will be our spokesperson?

A team flubs

What if the team is unable to complete its task, or the result of the team effort is not acceptable to the organization? This may seem like an unlikely possibility; but it is wise for a team to discuss in advance the eventuality their proposal, recommendation, or solution is not accepted. Imagining the scenario in which their best thinking would not be positively received can inspire a team to deeper, more thorough thinking about What haven't we thought of? Why would someone not endorse or affirm this plan? Where have we been wearing blinders as we have thought up our solution?

Inside Team: *I had a recent team experience in which we definitely succumbed to "groupthink." Over a period of a year, we brainstormed together; we thought up creative solutions to various elements of the need our team was trying to meet. We imagined ways the needs of the audience might be met. We refined our thinking and elaborated on our thinking, constructing detailed plans for the implementation of our team idea. When we took the idea to an outside group (after spending a great deal of time on "our idea"), the outsiders quickly took potshots at it. No, they shot a cannon-sized hole in the middle of our idea. They were a credible outside group we should have brought into the process earlier. We had been engaged in talking to ourselves and inspiring our-*

selves about our pet idea. People who had not been involved in the ideation had no difficulty pointing out flaws in our thinking, duplication of existing products, etc. We learned from their valuable input!

No purpose, no team

It may sound confining or narrow to equate the legitimacy of a team with its purpose. A group of individuals can certainly function and model the principles of teamwork without being a team. That is, a group can meet and be good listeners. They can be constructive in evaluating each other's viewpoints. They can have warm fellowship and be supportive of each other. They can share information and learn from each other. They can resolve differences of opinion smoothly and maintain esprit de corps. But, if they do not have a purpose which the members of the group can articulate and toward which the team is striving, in fact, the group is probably merely a group.

"A team is a group of people committed to a common purpose who choose to cooperate in order to achieve exceptional results."[3]

There are many groupings of individuals within the workplace and in organizations which are simply not teams: they have no identifiable purpose which binds them together. They may call themselves teams, and certainly there are no team police to demand they revise their name. Groups of individuals can embody the characteristics of a team, have a purpose, and produce high-level results, and not be aware or concerned about what they are called. They have an overarching purpose which is compelling to everyone involved. They are energized about moving toward their purpose. They hold themselves accountable for results. They are, in fact, operating as a team regardless of what terminology they use.

There are various terms which describe individuals who are nearly teams, including *working groups, pseudoteams, potential teams,* and others.[4]

A yardstick for determining whether a team is an authentic team is simply this: performance. Does the team have a purpose which is the essential springboard for goals? Are the goals measurable and thus indicators of whether the team has succeeded or not? This is the only test for a bona fide team.

Is everyone on the same page?

The team has come together for its initial meetings. The well-accepted stages of team development have begun: forming, storming, norming, and performing. Crafting of a team purpose statement has occurred. Team meetings begin to take on a certain life of their own. There are members who dominate the discussions because they are articulate or like to talk, and are quick thinkers and external processors. What about the team members who are less vocal? How can the team leader have a sense of whether each team member is affirming of the direction of the team?

One team consultant, Pat MacMillan, describes a concept called alignment.[5] Are all the team members rowing in the same direction? In the midst of all of the dynamics which are occurring in the meeting, it may be difficult to tell where each member stands. MacMillan recommends an alignment discussion be conducted one-on-one between the team leader and each team member. This conversation doesn't have to be lengthy; but particularly for new teams it enables the team leader to get a sense of where each member is. Is there something about the purpose the team has created which is foggy or even inexplicable to the team member? It takes boldness for a team member to voice, "I don't get it," particularly in a group setting. Does the team member feel this is the best purpose the team can have, that the direction the team seems to be headed is the most relevant and urgent path?

Three months into our organization's transition transformation to a team-based structure, I scheduled one-on-one conversations (recommended by MacMillan) with each team member. The discussions served a couple of purposes. Indeed some of the team members on the 2 teams I led were very reserved in the team meetings, saying virtually nothing. Having the alignment discussion enabled me to hear how they perceived we were doing as a team, particularly concerning purpose. A secondary purpose was achieved in enabling me to get acquainted with a few of the individuals who were new to the organization or with whom I had not worked before. A final benefit was the opportunity to hear to some of the emotional price tag which the organizational change was extracting from our staff. Several of the team members were candid in voicing how the change to teams had disrupted a strong existing department or group identity. As I listened, I heard the pangs of grief that these new team members were no longer a part of their former functional groups. They missed the camaraderie of being identified with people who performed the same function they did. Not only did we ask them to move their workplaces physically, the group they had felt kinship with and who understood each other was now scattered.

These were not results I had anticipated as part of the alignment discussions, but they did provide insights about individuals who were struggling to become members of a new team.

Individual function versus team purpose

A tension between the individual functions and the team purpose occurs among workplace teams more so than among temporary teams. The gravitational pull of doing "my job" first and foremost is strong. In the workplace, team members come to the team setting first as individuals. Secondarily, they are now asked to see themselves as team members. A lifetime of being graded and evaluated in terms of individual achievement in educational experiences and in the workplace makes it awkward to suddenly start operating collectively.

A mature workplace team is better equipped to navigate the waters in which individuals integrate their solo accountability with the team purpose. Mature teams have experienced some success in accomplishing together what the individuals cannot do on their own. The heady and satisfying feeling of accomplishment as a team creates the willingness to attempt even more challenging goals.

In the beginning of our organization's team odyssey, comments like "My plate is too full" or "I have a deadline" or "My schedule won't permit" were frequent. Team members were chafing at the challenge of balancing what they were responsible for individually with what they might have to contribute as a part of the team. Use of the words *my* and *I* were indicators the team members were viewing the work of the team as something layered on top of their individual functions. It is interesting to watch the gradual but sure steps of growth in teamship as the team begins to see "Our goal is to . . ."; "We can do . . ."; etc. A gradual pronoun shift to "our," "we need to," etc., indicates a buy-in from team members.

Inside Team: *Among the many teams within the Utopia Company was a hybrid called the Leadership Development Team. The stated purpose of the team was to advance not only skill development and learning among the entire resident staff but also to provide a plethora of external training opportunities which might ultimately provide a revenue stream and to foster the exploration of innovation both internally and externally. The small team delineated their individual functions with reasonable clarity: one team member was charged with internal training; another with external training; and the third staked claim to, for lack of a better term, a research and development function focusing on innovation.*

In the initial stages of their teaming, the tendency was for each of three core team members to merely report to each other what plans were on the horizon within her realm of responsibility: The strategy for staff development was shared. Plans for implementing several national training events were presented and discussed. The team member charged with innovation took care to feed her ideas about how the execution of the training initiatives could be strengthened.

Early in their team meetings, the team wrestled with the question, What could we do collectively that we cannot accomplish as individuals? The ballpark in which their team played was an immense one: training, leadership development, and innovation. Undergirding their discussions were the realities that revenue generation and market share of their company's customer base were important factors driving their team. How could what they did as a team provide meaningful and significant learning for inside audiences (staff) as well as external participants, and potentially contribute to revenue stream? And how could cutting-edge, innovative types of learning happen?

Because the team members established an atmosphere early on of free-floating creative exchange (and this creativity was strongly supported by other team members who were highly conceptual, visually oriented individuals, as well as administratively gifted), the team meetings were lively. Ideas were the coinage of their meetings. Still they wrestled with What one thing (or two things) could we establish as goals which only we could uniquely accomplish? And these goals must grow out of our team purpose.

Possibilities of writing a book together which would chronicle what the Utopia Company was learning in the midst of the megachanges it was undergoing organizationally was put on the table as one idea. Implementing existing plans for staff development and national training and even innovation training were going to go forward, regardless of the team. Each of these initiatives had a champion in one team member. The team still struggled with what their collective contribution would be.

Before the Leadership Development Team was six months old, a concept emerged which quickly became the goal for their first year: create a place within the company where ideas and creative thinking could be encouraged. Other companies had created large-group rooms, team centers, to give people the space to work, create, and socialize in a resource-rich environment with unique communication and creative thinking techniques.[6] The Leadership Development Team called their effort the DreamPort. Before the end of year one of the team's existence, it had designed, painted, furnished, and launched a large space within their company's building which would be open all the time to all employees for the purposes of stimulating their creative juices. Elements of the visual, the physical (a basketball game and a table tennis table), a place to sit and rest and think (comfortable sofas), a media corner, and a variety of creativity resources were all integrated.

Enjoying their success in the launch of the Dream-Port gave the team a vision for the kind of possibilities which they could accomplish collectively. Within the first year of the team's existence, the kernel of an idea for another goal took shape: what if the very building in which the Utopia Company existed became a center for learning for the constituencies which they were try-ing to reach? The team set about to describe in words the purpose of such a center, the kinds of learning models which would occur within its walls, and the actions which would need to occur to make it happen. During the second year of the Leadership Development Team's life, the goal they expressed involved position-ing the Utopia headquarters office setting as a center for learning. The team sketched out some pilot ven-tures which would introduce the Center for Mission Discovery and begin to establish its reputation, etc. The team was on its way!

Team Leader Technique: *A technique called alter-nately, clustering, mind mapping, and flapdoodling is a great way to generate ideas and/or explore an exist-ing idea.[7] Reduce the problem to a brief statement or a few words which you write in the center of a white-board, etc., with a circle around the words. Draw spokes out from the circle. As an association comes to mind, write it at the end of the spoke with a circle around it. Each circled idea is a starting point for thinking more deeply about a certain aspect of the original problem or issue. You can literally fill a wall with the associations which are prompted by the origi-nal statement or word. And looking at your ideas and information visually can enable you to see in the inter-relationships among the topics. Ideas never thought of before are likely to emerge.*

Processes Lead to Success

"There is no such thing as a natural touch. Touch is something you create by hitting millions of golf balls."[1]

How could anything as dull-sounding as a process be a significant factor in team success?

Simple. Process answers the key question that comes up repeatedly for a team: How do we . . .?

At the beginning of the team's formation and from that moment on, the team wrestles with implementing the actions which they have identified and agreed will enable them to accomplish their goal. As a reminder,

Purpose–Goals–Actions

Certain actions of the team may be like familiar refrains and keep resurfacing, such as how to

- develop a product, a tool, or a resource;
- plan an event, a training session, or a meeting;
- create a plan to market, communicate, or promote some element which the team has been working on;
- conduct a productive team meeting, focus group, or an input session;
- pay a bill.

Because these are the staples of team life in most organizations and because individuals from outside the team are often "players" in each process, it is helpful to map out these processes and to put them in writing. What's the first step? What are the subsequent steps which will lead to the desired outcome? Who is responsible for each action? What is the time frame for these actions?

It is important that each of the individuals who are expected to contribute to these implementation processes have access to the process as it is mapped out (often called a procedure). Someone has said it is in handing things off that we are most likely to fail.

Inside Team: *Opal was an experienced team leader in the XYZ Company. She had weathered numerous changes of top leadership. She was both observant and savvy about the cycles of activity which occurred in her company: an annual plan was a mainstay among the teams in XYZ Company. The development of detailed annual budget followed the annual planning. Strategic plans for a 2- to 5-year time frame were done periodically with assistance from the board of directors. Opal also paid attention to other recurring activities in which her team was expected to participate.*

Possessing a highly logical mind, Opal initiated the creation of documents which outlined the processes which affected her teams. She developed formats and made sure her team had access to all the forms. She took delight in assembling these processes in notebooks, along with the particular year's plan, budget, strategies, etc. She began to document other processes, and was proud of saying she "could be hit by a bus, but the work of her people would go on." Thanks to her written processes. She was partially right.

Several of her team members were less enthused about the unrelenting deadlines and demands for

written documents which described actions their unit
would do, followed by requests for revised documents.
The XYZ Company projected their planning for sev-
eral years in advance, so tracking the individual years
resulted in a voluminous output of paper. In fact, the
team members began to dread their leader's insatiable
desire for accumulating notebooks of plans. They com-
plained among themselves that these documents bore
a striking resemblance from year to year and a mini-
mal number of significant actions were actually being
carried out. They were too busy updating, revising,
and creating documents. One team member jokingly
threatened to create one strategic plan document and
keep resubmitting it with a new date on it each time
Opal asked for their latest plan.

What do you think? Can documenting plans or
creating procedures for recurring processes become an
end unto itself? Ask Opal.

The Big Four Thinking Processes

While processes which are the nuts and bolts in the execution of plans are important, equally significant are those
broad foundational processes which are common to all
teams. MacMillan refers to these as "thinking processes"
and notes these processes are most frequently ignored,
possibly because they sound and feel familiar.[2]

I want to focus on the "big four" thinking processes
which can spell the difference between failure and success
for a team. They are planning, decision making, problem
solving, and communication. The ironic thing about these
processes is they are familiar. Each team member already
has a variety of experiences, good, bad, and indifferent,
with each of these elements. A significant thing about the
nature of a process is learning or the sharpening of skills
happens within the context of the team. Teams collectively
can improve their planning, for example. They practice

this process on the playing field of their team meeting. A fledgling team, newly appointed, will be less able to create a thoughtful, practical plan than a team that has experienced being a team together for a couple of years.

Setting the stage for good processes

There is a single activity which, if done by a team in its early stages of development, can ensure the team will get off on the right foot with these important thinking processes: a team can develop thoughtful operating guidelines.

Called by various names, including the team covenant, operating principles, norms of the team, etc., this is a list of how the team agrees to behave when they are together, engaged in teamwork. Created by the team itself in a session which can be as brief as 30 minutes, each member has an opportunity to offer what he or she thinks is valuable as a standard in team behavior. When such a set of behaviors is created, everyone on the team holds everyone else accountable. Some teams post their guidelines in the meeting room to keep everyone equally mindful.

When my company transitioned to teams, the variety of ideas expressed as operating guidelines represented the diversity of the team membership. There were guidelines such as:

- We will celebrate at every meeting.
- We will start on time.
- We will always have an agenda (some even stipulated the agenda must be circulated 24 hours in advance).
- We will value each other's opinions.
- Silence means agreement.
- We will begin with prayer.

A good rule of thumb in response to How many should we create? is seven to ten statements expressed positively.

This number of guidelines will fit on a single sheet of paper and can be useful to the team. The team can choose at any time to review and revise the principles.

Several of the thinking processes, specifically communication, problem solving, and decision making, can be strengthened by including an operating guideline such as:

- Everyone has a right to an opinion in a discussion.
- We will not interrupt each other.
- We will strive to understand opposing viewpoints.
- We will attack the idea, not the person.
- There is no such thing as a stupid question or idea.
- We will keep team business at the team table.
- We will utilize straight talk.
- We will respect everyone's point of view

Once the team has crafted the principles by which they will operate, they move to discussions about the major processes which are common to all teams: planning, decision making, problem solving, and communication. The objective of such discussions is to acknowledge these processes as "big deals"; and as the team advances in the ease with which it is able to, for example, solve a problem, that team is destined for success.

Planning

"'For I know the plans I have for you,' declares the Lord, 'plans to prosper you and not to harm you, plans to give you hope and a future'" (Jer. 29:11 NIV) is one of my favorite planning verses. So much of what a team accomplishes can be traced back to whether they began with a plan.

How does a team jump into planning? Do they discuss planning first or simply begin to plan? In one sense, every time the team meets planning is occurring: discussions of issues related to the team unfold; ideas are generated;

potential approaches are explored. Since the team purpose is the glue which holds the members together, purpose is an excellent starting point for formal planning. What shall we do to ensure our purpose becomes a reality? When teams have spent sufficient time together to be able to express goals they are convinced will enable them to accomplish their purpose, then planning has begun.

As surely as a team sits down to plan, the team faces roadblocks in planning. A good team leader can be helpful in identifying the roadblock, checking the map, and suggesting an alternate route.

• An energized, ambitious team will surface numerous goals, and each goal has a series of actions necessary to bring it to completion. The actions can collide. What is the priority action? Each action has a team member's name associated with it and requires some work to be done. What if the team member fails to follow through? Team leader intervention: guide the team to limit itself to a manageable number of goals; and, as action plans are created, do a reality check on which team member is the champion of which action. Of course, the team leader's name should be there too. Has one team member optimistically overcommitted? One observer of team dynamics suggests a team engage in a periodic "chew-check." That is, has the team bitten off more than it can chew?[3]

• The team's agenda can be usurped by crises, unforeseen events, or the need to respond to a request for meeting time with another team. Frequently another team or individual in the organization may seek time with your team to explore an issue which relates to their work. Team leader intervention: the team leader is key in enabling a team to maintain its rhythm of spending appropriate time on planning. Charting the progress the team is making on completing actions, the team leader can suggest a course correction or facilitate a discussion with the team on the present reality. Are we going to be able to do this by our original date?

• When the team does not sense any progress is being made on the actions which they have identified as crucial, the morale of the team suffers. Team leader intervention: The team leader must keep an eye on actions which will qualify as short-term successes for the team. And, the team leader must be unafraid to revisit the approaches or methodology which the team had originally suggested. Is this still the best or only way for our team to accomplish this goal?

Maintaining focus in planning is the team leader's domain. Limiting the number of goals a team tries to tackle simultaneously can enhance planning. The pursuit of goals is an ongoing activity for a team. When one goal is accomplished and checked off as complete, then another one moves into focus.

The authors of *The New Why Teams Don't Work* suggest a simple way for dealing with the overflow of goals and actions which teams are likely to create. Sort them according to one of three time frames.[4]

Short—less than one month.
Mid—one to three months.
Long—three to six months.

There is something refreshing about a team considering what they are going to do in the next 30 days to further their purpose. There are obviously things which can and ought to be done in the next 30 days. When a team has taken the time to categorize all of their potential goal into these time frames, when the 30 days are ended, they should be able to recognize the completion of some actions. It's then appropriate to look in their midrange actions and transfer some of those into the next short-range time frame, etc.

It is important to remember that the team plans. While the team leader has a role in planning and can help a team stay on track in the process, the team leader does not own or initiate the plan.

Most teams have members who may approach planning in a couple of very different styles. One is the Big Picture person who presses for the general direction and outcome. Period. Seated across the table is the detail person who raises a laundry list of questions about exactly how the plan will unfold, when, and where, etc. A challenge for the team as a whole is to include enough detail in the plan to satisfy those who need everything spelled out and not to lose the individuals who care primarily about the broad strokes of the plan. Team leaders can point out this difference in style as a lesson that diversity strengthens a team. Both types of thinking about planning are valuable. Diverse teams are strong teams.

Decision making

The very lifeblood of a team meeting is the give-and-take discussion which is generated as the team members gather to do the real work of their team. Propelled by their purpose and headed toward goals which will allow them to measure their success, teams reach crossroads in their journey. At times these crossroads occur multiple times in the same meeting. At a point in a free-flowing discussion it becomes apparent the team must make a decision. How does the team come to grips with an issue on which different team members have viewpoints which are poles apart?

The issue may be one of making a choice between Plan A or Plan B. There are proponents of both plans on the team. Several have spoken with clarity on behalf of one plan or the other. The team cannot implement both. Which will it be?

If the team merely turns to the team leader to make the call, expediency may reign; but the team gives up the opportunity to work through the decision collectively. At a point in the future, the team may look back at "Betty's decision."

Decision making by team takes time, particularly if the team is doing more than simply voting on which of the two plans seems best. If possible, team leaders should be reluctant to ask their teams to vote as a means of making decisions. Though efficient, the team members are quickly cast into two opposing camps—a polarization into "them" and "us." And teams have a habit of remembering who was on which side. Growth toward a sense of team can be quickly eroded.

Given time for adequate discussion and surfacing the pros and the cons of each plan, often the team is able to collectively see and agree upon which course of action is best.

Consensus decision making is a term commonly used to describe the process when these conditions exist. This process is aided by individuals on the team whose contribution is to recap or summarize the major points of difference between the potential solutions. If clarity about the implications of a decision does not exist, then the team often resorts to seeking an outside expert who can bring the needed clarity. In any case, the team is still in the driver's seat in terms of making the decision.

I heard a team leader describe a novel technique called Fist-to-Five. When a decision has been sufficiently explained by a team member, the whole team is given the opportunity to express support, or lack of support, by using one of their fists (not in a battle with other team members). Simply, each team member displays a fist for the rest of the team to see. Meaning is assigned as follows:

- Closed fist: a no vote. A way to block consensus. I need to talk more on the proposal and require changes for it to pass.

- One finger: I still need to discuss certain issues and suggest changes that should be made.
- Two fingers: I am more comfortable with the proposal but would like to discuss some minor issues.
- Three fingers: I'm not in total agreement but feel comfortable to let this decision or a proposal pass without further discussion.
- Four fingers: I think it's a good idea/decision and will work for it.
- Five fingers: It's a great idea and I will be one of the leaders in implementing it.[5]

If a team used this technique and a decision prompted several closed fists or only one or two fingers of support, then the team would be well advised to continue to discuss its options.

Even after a decision is made, and particularly if the decision is one which has significant implications, a team leader may choose to follow up with a "second-chance" meeting.

Inside Team: *Shortly after a team retreat in which the management of our company had turned the existing organizational hierarchy upside down by creating a team-based structure, the CEO called a morning meeting of those who had been on the retreat. She only asked one question: "Have you had any misgivings about the decision we made at the retreat? You've had a chance to sleep on it. Do you still think this is the right and best decision for us?" The entire group affirmed the new team direction, and within hours all employees were briefed on the direction the company would be going. If any team member had voiced reservations, or second thoughts, then a deeper exploration discussion would have been necessary.*

Problem solving

A must in solving a problem is to identify exactly what the team is trying to solve. In the context of a church, a group of leaders charged with congregational vitality must dig a little deeper than merely observing, "Our problem is we're in a slump." A company selling mops has to do better than state, "Our problem is our mops aren't moving." A team in charge of its company's customer service has to pursue a problem that goes beyond "Our problem is our cranky customers." The more the team is able to be specific about the nature of the problem, root causes of the problem, history of this problem occurring in the past, etc., the more likely the team is able to zero in on what they are trying to solve.

Often, "the problem" can be broken down into a subset of problems. Each element of the problem requires a series of actions to bring resolution. Various pieces of the problem may require research or input from other sources in order to fully understand the scope of the problem. As in decision making, the team must spend adequate time in discussion to surface nuances of the problem. When multiple root causes have brought the problem into existence, the team will want to determine a priority of attack: which problem first? It seems clear that decision making and problem solving go hand in hand as the team navigates through the waters of problems confronting the team.

Team composition (i.e., the types of personalities who are team members) will shape the problem-solving process. Gregarious, outspoken team members may quickly assert, "The problem is . . ." in an emphatic tone of voice. Quieter, more reflective team members, who need time to process what others are saying, may not say as much in the initial discussion. Everyone on the team has ideas and opinions. The challenge for a team leader is to create space for everyone to make his or her contributions.

How does a team get a wide spectrum of ideas on the table as discussion ensues about either the greatest problem facing the team or the possible solutions? Two techniques which have a track record for enabling creative contributions from team members are brainstorming and the nominal group technique.

Team members may or may not have a level of familiarity with both techniques. In any case, describing the "rules" for using the technique establishes level ground for all team members:

- **Brainstorming**. With someone enlisted to capture ideas on a flip chart/whiteboard, the team leader facilitates a session in which the objective is to surface as many potential ideas as possible on the subject (i.e., What is the problem we're facing? or What's one approach we might use to address our problem?). Specify a time frame for the brainstorming ("For the next 27 minutes, we're going to . . ."; and even using the gimmick of a timer to keep on track often adds to the experience) or the number of ideas you'd like the team to generate. No idea suggested is critiqued or discussed as it is suggested. Encourage piggyback ideas to increase the pool of ideas generated. At the end of the brainstorming time, the team can evaluate the ideas by selecting their top three choices, combine several ideas to create a new thought, etc.

- **Nominal group technique.** In most teams, the quick-thinking talkers may dominate a brainstorming session. Yet, others on the team have worthy suggestions to offer. This idea-generating approach begins with the facilitator setting the scene or focus for the team and setting the time frame. Each team member then silently brainstorms, jotting down as many responses to the topic as he or she can think of. The facilitator can then use a flip chart to record responses, going round-robin around the group so each member can offer his or her unique responses one at a time. Following the input, the team can vote on the top choices, much as in a brainstorming session. (Hint: Often using self-stick notes to "vote" is a change of pace and enables a quickly visible way to see which ideas have garnered the most votes.)

Communication

Although each of the "big four" processes is essential for the success of a team, communication is a common, critical thread which winds its way through the other three. In fact, there is great overlap between the critical processes. The challenge in mastering the processes occurs simultaneously with the doing of what the team has defined as its work: taking steps to accomplish its purpose.

A wise team remembers communication is a multifaceted process. A team can always expand or deepen its skills in this complex arena. The number of factors which make up the larger topic of communication is extensive: oral and written communication, body language, gender communication issues, presentation skills, to mention a few. Too, there is vast literature both scholarly and popular on communication, as well as academic degrees in this discipline. How can a team get a handle on this broad topic?

Is it possible to isolate one or two key elements of communication as more significant than the rest? Probably not. Yet in the context of a team, two aspects of communication rise to the surface: listening and conflict resolution. A team which cultivates the habit of listening to each other and is able to identify and handle conflict is miles ahead of the team which delicately sidesteps differences, choosing harmonious, agreeable discussions as their primary goal. A team which has a poor track record in listening to each other and/or which fails to deal with conflict is probably headed for failure as a team.

Earlier I referred to the thoughtfulness with which a team approaches the creation of operating principles as a factor in placing the team in a win-win situation when communication snafus erupt. Listening to each other respectfully can become a habit which shapes the culture of the team. Refraining from interrupting or resorting to smirks or eyeball rolling in reaction to a fellow team member's ideas pays off for the team as a whole. Members who perceive a sense of safety within the team environment may voice a seemingly zany idea that the team can refine into a great idea.

Every team will eventually wind up in conflict. And the more quickly the team identifies opposing viewpoints on the issue and takes action to sort through the implications of each viewpoint, the stronger the team will be. Conflict is a natural occurrence among people who represent diverse thinking styles, different functional expertise, cultural backgrounds, etc. When a team floats along without conflict, it is likely some team members are holding back, not expressing their opinions, and going along with the majority. The emergence of conflict and the manner in which a team addresses their differing opinions enables a team to grow. Conflict is survivable. When conflict surfaces, the team has the opportunity to test skills and techniques which will enable them to resolve conflict more quickly in the future.

We've listened to each other and we don't agree!

Often the team leader plays a primary role in conflict resolution, although anyone on the team has the potential of making a vital contribution, particularly if the team leader is one of the parties engaged in conflict.

The basics of resolving conflict are straightforward: First someone is bold enough to identify that "we seem to be in conflict here." This step may seem an obvious one, but teams have spent unnecessarily long hours discussing an issue without making significant progress until someone spoke up and called the conflict what it was. Advocates for one action are given an opportunity to describe their viewpoint. Advocates for the other possible action are given a similar opportunity. The team leader seeks clarity of each viewpoint for the sake of the team.

One novel approach to test whether one side has genuinely heard the viewpoint of the other side is to ask a team member who advocates Plan A to express the gist of Plan B. Those who favor Plan B can then say, "You've got it! That's our plan!" Then, a team member who is a proponent of Plan B has an opportunity to present the salient points of Plan A. Has that member grasped the significant rationale for Plan A?

In the course of discussing each side, it is often helpful to clarify the pros and the cons which taking one action or the other would bring about.

Team Leader Technique: *Lead your team in a simulated decision-making process by describing a survival scenario such as: "You're leaving for the Great Smoky Mountains tomorrow for an indefinite period of time. What eight items will your team take from among the following which would ensure your survival in this locale? (Include blanket, map, cellphone, 50 feet of rope, waterproof tarp, insect repellent, sunblock, rain slicker, shovel, hiking boots, dehydrated food (six meals), CD player, illustrated guide of edible plants, gloves, knife, lantern, compass, first-aid kit, lip balm, fishing pole, water jug, hat, hand mirror, snakebite kit, twine, toilet paper, matches, camp stove, flashlight, change of clothes, rowboat) Give the team members a time frame (at least 20 minutes for discussion). As team leader you may want to observe the team dynamics, then discuss with the team how they came to their decision on which items to take.*

Culture Is Unique

"Culture is a little like dropping an Alka-Seltzer into a glass—you don't see it, but somehow it does something."[1]

The dictionary defines culture as a set of shared attitudes, values, goals, and practices that characterize an entity.

Not every group of individuals who sit through meetings together, communicate in the same language, and share common interests, actually develop into a team. Nor should they be expected to do so. Likewise the label of team may be foisted on a group of individuals, and yet they lack the basic elements which make a diverse group of people a team.

Inside Team: *A group of women leaders representing regional chapters of their national organization meet together several times each year. They share much in common, including educational backgrounds and generational similarities. They implement similar programs in their respective areas of the country. They are deeply committed to the aspirations of their national organization and energetically promote its mission. During their sessions each year, an outside observer might note the warm sense of camaraderie which permeates the room. Their intense conversations and storytelling are punctuated by laughter and mutual interest. They are eager to learn from each other, "What's working in your area?" When the meeting concludes, there is a sense of regret on the part of the participants. Does this group of women constitute a team? No. Though they share involvement in a national organization, each woman is very connected to her region. Though information, motivation, and learning experiences flow back and forth, their national identity is loosely structured. There are no specific goals which demand their collaborative efforts. Their differences are as notable as what they have in common.*

The main stumbling block is there is no compelling reason for them to act collaboratively. They have no joint vision or goal which they can only accomplish by the women from the West Coast and New England "pulling together." Without that glue, the women maintain their professional relationship as colleagues and even friends, but there is little to propel them beyond this relationship.

What are the distinctive hallmarks of the culture of a group of individuals who act as a team? What do they value collectively and how does it play out in their shared life? What, beyond the operating guidelines of a team, is reflective of its culture? Each team has a distinctive culture. There may or may not be conscious effort on the part of the team to define, describe, or understand its culture. The culture exists, nonetheless, and can be examined by a thoughtful look at a team's

- reason,
- rhetoric,
- roles,
- rhythm,
- relationships.

Reason: Why does the team exist?

The reason for a team's existence is often called its purpose, or mission. The clarity which surrounds What are we doing? and Why are we doing this? is a foundational element in the growth of a team.

A writing teacher I once had encouraged me to take the "fog index" out of my writing. A team must look at their core purpose from every imaginable angle to extract meaning from it. If ambiguity, or a fog index, clouds why the individuals have come together in the first place, then it is likely the team will flop.

Teams which exist in an organization as well as volunteer teams in any setting must wrestle with this question. The answer may be very accessible and be spelled out in a charter, mandate, or assignment which was handed off to the team when they were created. An entrepreneurial team, on the other hand, has the freedom of crafting their own mission statement. They start with a clean slate.

While reason is the significant thing which a team must determine, at the same time it is also only a set of words which guides the direction of the team. As such, there is little cause for a team to make a career out of crafting, revising, perfecting, and polishing a perfect statement of their purpose. The team may state their purpose in terms of solving a problem, or meeting a need, or bringing about a particular outcome. When the team accomplishes the purpose, if the team is ongoing, it moves to its next purpose. If the team has been brought into existence for the precise reason it has now accomplished, the team is ready to disband.

When my organization transitioned from a traditional department-based structure to teams, I noticed the groups who knew why they existed and what they were expected to do labored over capturing their purpose in just the right terminology. Often the teams' purpose statements were lengthy, an attempt to spell out too much of what they were to do.

A simple declarative statement of "Our team exists to . . ." is easier for team members to remember and to take action on than a page of complex verbiage.

Individual team members may bring differing levels of enthusiasm to the team purpose. As noted in chapter 4, a leader role is to discern and discuss with team members their willingness to be engaged with the team purpose. While some team members will be wholehearted in their understanding and belief in the reason the team exists, others may be neutral or reluctant to endorse the purpose. Team culture dictates whether those differences of perspective are openly discussed. Successful teams are frequently teams that maintain an open dialogue about urgency of their purpose.

Their team culture implies what we're about is important to us individually and as a team. We want to succeed. And here's our plan for success.

Rhetoric: How does the team sound?

Communication is a major factor in team success. An outsider in a team meeting can often pick up on the vitality of a team by listening and watching the interactions between team members.

A team which demonstrates these signs is on a healthy team path:

- Participation in the team conversation by all team members
- No dialogue hogs (i.e., there's a give-and-take to the discussion among all the team members)
- Moments of levity or laughter
- Open differences of opinion (conflict)
- Respectful listening to all team members
- Willingness to ask questions when issues or meanings are unclear

- Awareness and appreciation that individuals on the team have different functional accountabilities
- Seamless shifting among those whose expertise varies greatly
- Energetic exchanges of opinions
- Team vocabulary which all team members have in common
- Consensual decision making
- Use of *we* and *our*
- Skilled facilitation by the team leader
- Agreement of what is to be reported from the team and who will do it

Consider the rhetoric of each of these teams:

Inside Team: *The mission of the Green Thumb Company is to produce accessories and tools for the home gardener. Several teams within the company are involved in suggesting designs for innovative products. One team, composed of a cross section of staff, is charged with evaluating all new products and determining which product has the highest potential and would be the best use of Green Thumb's total resources. Kathy leads the evaluation team. She also is a member of a team which frequently submits product ideas.*

Following a recent meeting, several members of the evaluation team voiced concerns to each other that the ideas generated by Kathy's team are usually presented as fait accompli rather than as proposals to be evaluated. While other product ideas are thoroughly hashed out, those from Kathy's team are presented and, under her strong leadership, approved.

As a member of the evaluation team who noticed this recurring pattern of product approval, what action could you take? How would you broach the subject?

Inside Team: *In one company's across-the-board reorganization, every group that had once been a department became a team. There were several individual contributors who did not seem to fit on any newly formed team. Management decided to cluster those individuals on a single team and let them come to grips with their purpose and direction for the future. The individuals who comprised the team were strong leaders and knowledgeable about their particular function. Their leader was a long-term staff member committed to the success of the team.*

After meeting for over a year, the team's purpose statement appeared to be a cut-and-paste compilation of those functions which each team member carried out. Conversation on the team often centered on sharing the individual's goals and direction. The team continued to struggle with what they could do or should do collectively.

As the team leader, what path or approach would you take to enable this team to succeed? Is this team a bona fide team? Should it try to be?

Inside Team: *The Customer Relations Team of a publishing company was challenged by management to begin actively selling product to customers who called in to place an order. This was a challenging new venture for the team. Training occurred. During a time of goal setting, the team was attempting to establish sales quotas for individuals and the team as a whole. The team leader had asked an outsider to facilitate the session in which the goals were established. At the end of the session, the leader was less than excited about the low target goals which were set. The team members, unfamiliar with and nervous about selling during customer calls, had set their quotas very low.*

As the discussion facilitator, what could you have done to influence the goal setting? As the team leader,

*at the table during the discussion, what might your
action have been?*

Roles: Who does what?

A newly formed team within any company, or a group of
volunteers who have been given a task, represents a variety of roles. At first glance, team roles can be viewed simply in terms of who are the members? Who is the leader?
These are the formal roles which most teams share.

Exploring a little deeper, the team becomes aware of
different functions or technical expertise existing within
the membership of the team. A cross-functional team may
have an engineer, a salesperson, a graphic designer, an
editor, a financial person, etc. On a volunteer team in a
local church, one may have similar functions represented
and unearth even wider diversity. A recent church team
experience I had threw together a hospital chaplain, a high
school science teacher, two college professors (one nursing,
the other Spanish), a child psychiatrist, an antique store
clerk, and me.

The more diverse the functional expertise on the team,
the stronger the team is as it comes to grips with its purpose.

In addition to the variety of functional expertise which
is identifiable among team members, there are numerous
roles which team members adopt and fluidly move in and
out of. These are positive roles which enhance team development and accomplishment of its purpose. There are also
roles which have a negative impact on the team. Among
corporate training events, there is a distinct reason for the
popularity of seminars which focus on dealing with difficult people.

It is possible that a team member may exhibit behaviors which work against the best interests of the team.
Many books on teams have categorized these types at

length, including a creative list from *The New Why Teams Don't Work*.[2] The authors describe:

- The team jerk
- The team brat
- The team blowhard
- The negative thinker
- Dark angels

The authors also suggest strategies which the team leader can plan in advance to counterbalance the actions of a less-than-constructive team member.

The most important role which a member plays often boils down to what that member is willing or able to do to move the team toward the accomplishment of its purpose. As the team deliberates upon its task, goals are established and actions are identified which will lead to the accomplishment of the goal. Who will fulfill a particular action? What recourse does the team have if no one on the team has the skill or ability to fulfill that action?

During my church team experience, described earlier, we had occasion to implement a congregational survey. As the results came in, the question of who would compile or tabulate the many survey results. As is often the case on diverse teams representing a variety of professionals, one of our members volunteered that she had survey software on her computer which could make quick work of the task. Her contribution then was one of furthering the larger team purpose. It was a significant contribution!

Everyone on the team (including the leader) has the potential for a real work chore. I sometimes refer to the "grunt work" which grows out of a team assignment. While much of a team task may consist of discussion, generating ideas, analyzing options, strategizing, making plans, etc., a need may arise for research and research compilation, painting a floor, packing boxes, stuffing envelopes, moving furniture, cleaning up after a meal function, etc. Each of these roles are within the realm of carrying out the team task.

Inside Team: *In a recent training session for team leaders, teams of four were introduced to a survival simulation scenario called Black Bear.[3] The setting was the Great Smoky Mountains and the challenge was to make a quality decision in a crisis situation. The exercise was timed. Several of the teams had individuals on their team who were familiar with hiking in the mountains. One team consisted of four individuals who had no experience or previous knowledge about the mountain setting, the gear, or the challenges of the wilderness.*

At the conclusion of the exercise, only half of the teams were successful in accomplishing their team purpose. The team which had no "expert" role among their members was one which was successful. In debriefing, they attributed their success to their early acknowledgement that they were total wilderness novices, had no wisdom born of experience, and their only path to success was to understand the scenario thoroughly and use their best logic and intuition as a team in crafting a solution. Another team who had several seasoned hikers on their team quickly devised their solution to the simulation, relying on the opinion of their experts, and failed to accomplish synergy as a team.

Having individuals on the team who were acknowledged experts did not ensure the success of the team. This same principle is true in considering roles on a team. The collective IQ of a team, which necessitates getting maximum input from all the team members, is a powerful team dynamic.

Rhythm: How does the team get anything done?

A team may move rapidly, or at a snail's pace, toward the accomplishment of its purpose. Movement occurs because the team identifies the steps it will need to take in order to bring about its unique purpose.

A major contribution which a team leader delivers to the team is to enable the team to remain focused on its direction. Most often, the team makes strides in its purpose because the team is willing to engage in thoughtful planning. Planning is a process which is a nuts-and-bolts essential for a team. The team leader can facilitate the team in planning what needs to happen, in what order, and by when in order for the desired end result to occur. Teams which have spent time together have developed their planning expertise and skills. It is good to note creating the plan and executing the plan are crucial.

Planning is hardly a mysterious discipline. Anyone who goes into a supermarket with a shopping list has developed a plan. Once the shopper is inundated with all the possible sales and free samples in the market, sticking to the list is another challenge.

Following a clear understanding of the team purpose, a path for accomplishing that purpose is discussed by the team. The distractions which a team may face after the purpose has been articulated are the variety of approaches which the team might take toward its purpose. If a team is particularly diverse, many rabbits may be pursued during the purpose discussion.

The purpose is usually divisible into smaller, bite-sized pieces called goals. Once a team has goals, it has established a means by which it can measure its progress. A team leader's role in keeping the team focused and establishing a pace or rhythm is valuable here. It is possible for a team can derail itself through:

- intriguing but nonessential discussions;
- spending time implementing activities which do not lead toward one of their goals;
- being overly laid back about what must happen during a critical time frame;
- unrealistic budget expectations (if a goal is dependent upon an expensive piece of research, what is Plan B?);
- underestimating the demands of individual accountabilities and their impact on the work of the team.

If no one else on the team is conscious of the rhythm or pace at which a team works, the team leader must keep the beat. The leader can do this by

- making sure that what the team spends time on during their meeting is relevant to the team purpose;
- surfacing those broad areas in which planning is needed;
- creating an environment and a time frame in which planning and execution of the plan can occur (it's hard to produce good team results when the meeting is one hour every other month);
- assimilating what is being said and decided by the team, and keeping that message in front of the team (thus the team doesn't have to rehash what it decided in an earlier meeting).

Relationships: How do they get along?

For members of some teams, the very idea that they do not have to be best friends with fellow team members in order to be successful is a liberating one. The team has been set into motion for a purpose: the individuals who comprise membership may be great comrades, or they may only have their team involvement in common.

Of the many possible hallmarks of good relationships on teams, several rise to the top. I particularly resonated with the list suggested by Pat MacMillan in *The Performance Factor*. He suggests a group of individuals who can exhibit these six characteristics are well on their way to becoming a team: trust, understanding, acceptance, respect, courtesy, and mutual accountability.[4]

Often the exercise in which operating guidelines are crafted is a productive opportunity for these key principles to be addressed. For example, an operating guideline which stipulates "Conversations about team business will remain at the team table" enables team members to speak openly without the fear their remarks will be misunderstood outside of the team discussion context. This guideline is not so much about confidentiality, but about the team members being able to trust that their thoughts will be kept within the context of the team.

Other operating guidelines which may promote these foundational relationship principles might include the following:

- All questions will be viewed as an opportunity to learn.
- Discussion will continue until clarity is achieved.
- Everyone's ideas and opinions will be treated with respect.
- All team members deserve courtesy.
- We are accountable to each other to adhere to our guidelines.

What do these principles look like in the context of a team meeting?

Characteristic	It exists when	It's missing when
Trust	Team members speak candidly to each other, divulging opinions or questions which have the potential for being misunderstood.	Team members assume a detached or uninvolved stature; conversations are prefaced with "This must be confidential"; etc.
Understanding	Following discussion, a team member's face lights up with comprehension; a team experiences a team-building exercise in which team members begin to know and appreciate each other in new ways.	Team members tune out when another team member offers a technical explanation; team members exhibit impatience with a fellow team member who processes information internally.
Acceptance	Team members from widely different backgrounds or experiences affirm the contribution on each other.	A team member's opinion is discounted because his cultural orientation is different. ("Fred just doesn't get it. . . . They don't do it like that in New York!")

Characteristic	It exists when	It's missing when
Respect	Team members pay as much attention to the youngest, newest, least-positioned team member as they would to the boss of the company.	Team members interrupt or talk over each other; roll their eyes at another's contribution.
Courtesy	Team members have developed the habit of being polite with each other even when processes like communication and problem solving take more time than they had anticipated.	Team members engage in cutting remarks, often at the expense of a team member who is absent; humor is pointed and often deprecating.
Mutual Accountability	There is a sense of candor and collegiality about progress toward team goals; there is a willingness to be interdependent.	Team members are touchy about their areas of expertise; they tend to be defensive when the team gives input.

The culture of a team evolves. Each aspect of team behavior and interaction, and the result they are able to produce, is on a path of growth. The more time a team spends on the playing field of meeting together addressing their team purpose, the more likely the team will succeed.

A noticeable change occurred within an organization with which I am familiar. It transitioned from functional departments to teams. At an initial meeting of team leaders to share team goals shortly after the change had been implemented, the discussion was territorial and protective of their individual team territory. Over a period of 2 years of practicing teamwork, the same team leaders spent an extended amount of time together again sharing goals and team information. The spirit of this meeting was marked by growing familiarity with good team practices, including the benefit of integrating goals from all of the teams. As each team leader shared goals from his team, a lively atmosphere of piggybacking ideas from other team perspectives occurred. Affirmation of the direction in which a team was headed and creative ways that one team could help another were the norm of this meeting.

Team Leader Technique: *To promote team learning, invite a different team member at each meeting to be responsible for providing a learning moment for the whole team. That team member will share at the beginning of the meeting a two- to three-minute intriguing idea or concept that he read about in a newspaper, magazine, book, or found on a Web site. Limiting the time frame keeps the report concise. The individual may even want to bring a copy of the article for the team. Inviting team members to apply the idea to the work of the team can lead to new team resourcefulness.*

A parallel idea is to provide a plastic toolbox (or colorful bag) of idea-provoking toys such as a fuzzy rubber ball, building blocks, bubbles and wand, kalei-

doscope, play dough, crayons, modeling clay, spring
toys, etc. When the team needs a little stress relief or a
"tool" to inspire their thinking, the toolbox will provide
the thinking aid!

Meetings

"There were board meetings when my wife was doing needlepoint, one sister was addressing Christmas cards and another didn't bother to attend."[1]

Why meetings?

"What? Not another meeting?"

"If I didn't have so many meetings, I could get my work done."

"Well, that was a waste of time."

"I may have a headache the next time this group schedules a meeting."

"I don't know any more now than when the meeting began."

Do any of these statements sound familiar? A few unique and hardy souls may actually welcome meetings. Perhaps their esteem needs are met by chalking up hours in meetings they have been asked to attend. Others complain or whine about the time which meetings take compared to the value of what they accomplish.

Once upon a time, an organization for which I worked had a deeply rooted cultural norm related to meetings. For years, the company designated an entire week each month during which staff travel was discouraged, and being available for meetings was a priority. As the staff grew to over

100, scheduling the meetings became a tedious, complex labor. Particular staff members were required participants in a majority of the meetings. An administrative assistant spent hours each month coordinating one master schedule which juggled all the requests for time, personnel, and rooms. She then distributed a multipage document, typically on pink paper, which ruled for that week. Meeting days began early and ended late to accommodate all the demands for meetings. Staff members complained, tongue-in-cheek, "I only have 42 hours of meetings this week." Most meetings resulted in follow-up actions which the same meeting attendees had to find time to implement.

Today, this company still has meetings, but they are spread out over the entire month. The staff no longer relies on a master schedule. The dreaded week-of-meetings marathon has ended. How did the change occur? An observant and compassionate supervisor took pity on the administrative assistant whose job it was to create the schedule. She inquired, "Isn't there another way we can handle meetings?" Discussion ensued, but the ultimate answer was yes. Those who call meetings can schedule them. Only occasionally is a staff member, frustrated about trying to gather the appropriate players for a session, heard to pine, "I wish we would return to the way we used to do meetings."

A seven-letter word, *meeting,* which ought to be fairly neutral, can take on a connotation of dread and avoidance. Its mere mention in some workplaces, organizations, and even the church prompts snide remarks and eye rolling. Each of these entities do work by small group, whether it is called a team, a task force, or a committee. Meetings are the most common vehicle by which a group does its work, a necessary element of working collaboratively. MacMillan has called meetings the playing field on which the team plays.[2]

Meetings have the potential for being lively, productive, and even fun; but only if the meetings are necessary and planned well.

Planning for meetings

The number one factor in delivering a successful meeting is a well-constructed, thoughtful agenda circulated in advance of the meeting. The agenda assures that team members are not surprised by topics on which they are expected to make a contribution. They are given a heads-up about materials they might need to bring to the meeting. It is also the surest tool of the team leader to help the team focus and make progress on goals related to their purpose.

Many of the teams in my workplace have adopted an operating guideline which simply says, "No agenda, no meeting." No team in our organization has expressed the need for refreshments as a regular part of the meeting. When the team is celebrating a milestone or accomplishment, a refreshment or treat is appropriate. Or should the timing of the meeting run into the lunch hour, a dish of snacks might be appreciated.

The meeting planner, frequently the team leader, creates the agenda. She begins by considering a series of questions including, Why are we meeting? What does the team need to accomplish during this meeting? Beyond the team, are there additional people who need to be involved in order for the team to accomplish its purpose in the meeting? What is a reasonable time frame for this activity to happen?

As one who frequently plans meetings, I include on the agenda an approximate number of minutes I anticipate spending on a given topic, along with the name of the responsible team member. In a meeting with a new team, I asked them, "What did we do well today?" at the end of the meeting. I was gratified to learn the team felt the agenda contributed to their productivity. I also received a bit of unexpected insight when one of the team candidly commented I (as facilitator) was very wed to the agenda and she, for one, needed more time to process the information before being asked to make a decision. A point well taken.

An agenda is more than listing the location, participants, and time of the meeting. The topics included on a purpose-driven agenda are more than a compilation of individual input from team members who need the team to address an issue or who want to share information with the team. A guiding principle in crafting an agenda is to ask, "What is the one thing which we must do in the meeting today?" List that item as number one. This ensures that if the discussion is punctuated by digressions or somehow derailed, at least the first item is covered. Anyone who regularly calls meetings and greets the participants with a cheery, "What shall we talk about today?" mentality will find the participants' enthusiasm, and probably meeting attendance, will wane. Also, team members appreciate a team leader who cancels a meeting when she has recognized there is no compelling reason to meet.

I often rely on a handy tool, the agenda template, included as part of the Microsoft Word software. I can quickly format and email an agenda to multiple individuals on-site or off-site.

Where and when to meet are often dictated by available space and availability of the team members. A comfortable room with adequate space for the entire team is essential. A room which will accommodate the type of meeting you are planning is another factor. If your team is expected to spend several hours in a brainstorming session, it may be best to have space to move around. And often it is enhanced by whiteboards, wall space for flip chart pages, and/or floor space for easels. Some teams express a preference for doing creative-type meetings in the mornings when they are fresher.

Successful meetings succeed because

- the right people are included at the table;
- there is clarity about what the team is expected to accomplish;

- necessary materials, documents, and information are available;
- the physical setting is conducive to team interaction (i.e., everyone can see and hear each other);
- the norms of the team are understood and respected;
- there is buy-in, or agreement, among the participants that the purpose of the meeting is important to the team.

Mediocre meetings are only mediocre because

- the purpose for the meeting was less than compelling/urgent and could have been handled in an email;
- one or more participants were allowed to be meeting hogs (i.e., monopolized the discussion);
- the meeting went overtime, with the most important item being rushed through at the end of the meeting;
- individual participants kept leaving the room to take phone calls, etc.;
- more rabbits were chased than significant issues dealt with;
- at the end of the meeting, no summary of decisions was expressed.

Meetings fail because

- perhaps the meeting should have never been scheduled to begin with;
- the facilitator lacked the skill to keep the meeting on track (i.e., managing the group processes such as communication, decision making, problem solving, and conflict resolution, while simultaneously paying attention to the task at hand);
- individuals who could have clarified and made contributions were not present;
- the meeting climate was tense with conflict which was never addressed or resolved;

- meeting participants had agendas which were never revealed to the large group;
- the norms of courtesy, respect, and clear communication were abandoned.

Facilitating the meeting

If the agenda is the number one tool which a team leader depends upon to lead a successful meeting, an essential skill the team leader relies on is facilitation.

One who facilitates simply makes the way easier for a team to come to grips with accomplishing its goals. Meetings run more smoothly and outcomes are more productive when a skilled facilitator is in the picture. The facilitator is often the leader of the team, but does not always have to be. Among teams in my organization, an idea has sprouted that all team members should be continually mentored and engaged in developing skills like facilitation. For that reason, many teams rotate the facilitation of the meeting among its members from meeting to meeting.

In the broadest sense, the facilitator's role is a balancing act between task and process. He or she pays attention not only to the progress the team is making toward the task established for the specific meeting but also is aware of how the team is accomplishing the task. Simultaneously, a good facilitator is mindful of the Big Picture (i.e., the meeting should be wrapped up by 3:00 P.M. with the next steps outlined by that time) and the dynamics of process (i.e., several of the team members seem to be a little cool to the idea which the rest of the team is ready to run with).

In my experience, good facilitators are keenly observant. They are attentive to the details of the physical setting of the meeting as well as the interactions between team members. Good facilitators are decisive and willing to take charge. When it's time to begin the meeting, regardless of who has not arrived, the facilitator begins, if only to make the rest of the team aware, "Larry hasn't made it to the meeting yet, but we're going to do XYZ which doesn't require his input." This is not to imply a facilitator is a boss or disciplinarian; but aware of her role as facilitator, she steps up to the expectation that she is expected to guide the team.

Facilitators are not driven by a need to be the expert on the issue confronting the team. In fact, if the team leader is aware she wants to be fully participative in the discussion, she would do well to delegate the facilitation to another team member or call in an outsider to serve in that role. It is highly unlikely a team member can champion a point of view, fully engage in discussion, and still function effectively as a facilitator. Facilitators often are wise to wear their hats of neutrality as a team debates the pros and cons of an issue. For an upcoming strategic directions session in my organization, both the executive leaders have chosen to enlist a facilitator who is not on the board or a senior executive. In this way, the top leadership can be fully engaged in the discussion without being hindered by serving as facilitators.

It sounds elementary to say a facilitator needs to be able to listen and think simultaneously. But the skill with which the facilitator can process what diverse team members are saying is crucial. This skill goes beyond simple feedback, which is valuable as well. At numerous junctures during the meeting, the facilitator sums up what has occurred so far, where the team is in the discussion, and what the next step might be. Often the facilitator is strictly summarizing, giving a play-by-play, of what the team members themselves have expressed. If the facilitator's assessment is not accurate, the team has the accountability to restate and clarify for everyone's benefit. Thus the team makes progress.

A facilitator is often very articulate and easily assimilates a variety of opinions. Synthesizing the direction in which the team is headed and testing the reality of implications that direction might involve is a facilitator's role. A facilitator is also one who is willing to pose questions, particularly if fellow team members are accepting of a direction without voicing relevant questions. It may be the team has chosen to wear blinders. The facilitator cannot.

A final characteristic of a facilitator is one which is primarily personality based, but can have great positive benefits when working with teams: a sense of humor. Often the tensions and accompanying conflicts which arise as a team solves problems, or discusses potential courses of action, are rooted in the depth of their passion about their team's task. Passion is good. Caring about the results of teamwork is good. Loyalty or commitment to the task is good. Tension, unresolved or ignored, is not good. A facilitator who has a lighthearted, humorous approach to inject into the discussion can alleviate a bigger problem. After all, the wisdom literature of Proverbs tells us laughter is a good medicine.

The role of a good facilitator cannot be underestimated in enabling a team or any other group to make decisions and therefore progress. A facilitator can also make a great contribution within a group which is not a team, per se. A whole organization, company, church, etc., can benefit from a skilled facilitator guiding their dialogue.

Inside Team: *Little Hollow Baptist Church was a small congregation pastored by a bivocational schoolteacher. He had been the leader since the formation of the church. His low-key teaching style of ministry was appreciated by most of the congregation. In fact, he was very respected and beloved by the congregation. Several years into the church's history, a few influential leaders determined a more dynamic pastor was essential for the growth of Little Hollow Baptist Church. Discussion about the fit of this particular pastor for the church at this point in its development began to surface.*

Shortly after the pastor became aware of the discussion among the members, he announced the following Sunday evening there would be an opportunity for a meeting and discussion by the church family. He enlisted a neutral member of the church to facilitate.

On the evening of the discussion, the facilitator set up flip charts in the church's small sanctuary. As the meeting began, she suggested a few meeting parameters such as the time frame and the basic issue which they were to discuss: Is our current pastor the best fit for Little Hollow at this time? The pastor had agreed to be present for the meeting or to remain in his study. The facilitator polled the church members who were present. They felt they could talk more freely in his absence.

The ensuing discussion consisted of complaints and descriptions about the pastor's preaching style and leadership. There were also glowing remarks about his dedication and humble spirit.

At the end of the discussion, no decision was made, but everyone had experienced the opportunity to voice their opinions. The facilitator had enabled the congregation to talk without resorting to using Robert's Rules of Order or being involved in a formal meeting. As she summed up what she had heard during the discussion, it was clear that two distinct camps of members were present: those who were satisfied with the current leader and those who were not. Several suggestions of ways the pastor could better serve the congregation were agreed upon by attendees (such as variety in the order of worship, for example). These suggestions were noted. Those who spoke of the need for a leadership change voiced the possibility they would seek a different community of faith for their families. The spirit of the meeting was a positive one in spite of the differences expressed.

In the months ahead, many of the suggested changes were made. The pastor remained in place. Several families began to visit other churches and eventually joined new congregations. Word of how this small community of faith had handled their differences spread and attracted new church members.

To Think About: *Would the outcome have been the same if the pastor had facilitated or if a church member who was clearly in one camp or the other had facilitated? What would have been the likely outcome if the pastor had not intervened as quickly as he became aware of the differences of opinion?*

Facilitation skill: enabling a group to decide

Much of what a team spends its time doing plays out in a few basic processes including planning, communicating, solving problems, and making decisions.

How a team makes decisions is a key process which a good facilitator can influence. A facilitator will enable a team to discuss, in advance of a decision, the common ways a group decides. The pros and cons of each solution will be laid out for all to see: The degree of involvement of the team in carrying out each method; the suitability of each method based on the particular decision to be addressed.

There are at least four common and identifiable methods of making decisions:[3]

- Command
- Consult
- Vote
- Consensus

Each method has its unique characteristics and appropriate uses within a team setting.

A command decision is one frequently made by outside forces and handed to a team:

- A decision to change the organizational structure
- A product price increase
- The schedule for an annual retreat
- Legislative enactments such as ADA (Americans with Disabilities Act), FMLA (Family and Medical Leave Act), etc.
- An IRS audit

The team, upon receiving the bottom line, has the challenge of how to proceed with their purpose and pursuit of goals in light of the decision under which they will now work. How can we move forward with this decision as our new parameter?

Inside Team: *A team which produced a monthly magazine was faced with reports of declining circulation. In an effort to contain costs, management decided the magazine would be printed on a less-expensive grade of paper. The team was called together and this decision was communicated. The response to the decision ranged from emotion on the part of those who perceived that total production quality was now negatively effected, to those who indicated a desire to proactively market the magazine in such a way to gain a wider market share. In any case, the command decision stood until circulation numbers improved.*

A second kind of command decision is one in which the decision is turned over to someone who is trusted. This may be a low stakes issue (such as where to have lunch today). And the team is comfortable letting someone else make the decision.

A decision may fall into the consult category when the team solicits the opinion of an individual who may have expertise not resident on the team. Or, the team may want broad-based input before making a decision. When seeking the input from others, a wise team discloses the input will not necessarily be the decision. But, the input will likely shape or inform the decision.

Inside Team: *A staff benefits team launched a process to explore new benefits which the company might offer. Through questionnaires and focus groups, various benefits were ranked by employees as highly desirable or least desirable. Although an in-house daycare was perceived as valuable to many employees, team analysis indicated that the benefit was not financially feasible. Instead, an alternative work schedule was introduced. Through careful communication at each juncture, the staff benefits team was able to roll out a benefit which was popularly received in spite of the fact it was not the first choice of the majority of employees who were consulted.*

Voting is a familiar means of narrowing down a field of potential solutions during a group decision-making process. The downside of voting among individuals who are team members is the "them" and "us" polarizing effect. Voting is efficient and can quickly reveal where people are in relationship to one decision option as opposed to another. If voting occurs openly, the team members' best judgment may be swayed by the vote of an influential fellow team member. If the voting occurs by secret ballot, the potential for polarizing is still in effect. To assure team solidarity, it is good to determine in advance whether a simple majority or a majority will determine the outcome of an issue put to a vote.

A final means by which a team might decide an issue is by consensus. This is an effective way to make decisions, providing a sufficient time frame exists to allow full discussion. Consensual decision making is time-consuming. It also requires skill from the facilitator in guiding the discussion. This method is also generally regarded as the best method to assure team buy-in.

The facilitator may want to remind the team members that as they strive to reach a consensual decision, there are "musts," or guidelines, for each team member, including the following:[4]

- Everyone must be as clear in stating his or her point of view as possible, adding as many facts to the information pool as he or she can.
- Everyone must be willing to listen to the reactions of the other team members.
- Everyone should avoid changing his or her mind simply to avoid conflict which may unfold during the team process.
- Everyone should resist the attempt to vote or average the number of people who support one solution over another.
- Everyone should be engaged in the discussion, with no sidelined members.
- Everyone should look for the best solution for the team.
- Everyone should resist the impulse to horse trade by giving in on one issue because a team member has supported your point of view on another issue in the past.

For more explanation on how a team reaches a consensus decision, see chapter 5.

Virtual team meetings

Technology has immensely expanded the horizons for teams. Organizations which invest in the necessary group work technology can empower individuals from different continents and time zones to be connected and collaborate on joint projects.

Such innovations as video, chat rooms, and teleconferencing are powerful tools for calling people together to address a common purpose. Email has made great strides in being the communication vehicle of choice for most organizations today. Document files are shared as quickly as pressing the Send command on the computer keyboard. Revisions and responses to ideas flow back and forth with ease. It is common to use threaded discussions in which an initial participant begins a conversation concerning an issue and other participants join the dialogue. The contributions of each are easily attributable and discussion occurs which enables the team to move forward on their purpose.

Those who have observed the use of technology and its impact on teams have noted there are both obstacles and opportunities for the virtual team.[5] While technology has allowed expanded access to people, reports, discussions, etc., the downside is the tendency to involve too many people. Just as 50 people in the same room, trying to function as a team would be hindered because of their sheer number, when virtual teams are expanded beyond the necessary participants, performance can suffer.

Another obstacle to virtual teams is the limitation groupware technology places on group creativity. There is no substitute for face-to-face interaction for maximum communication among teams.

With all of the pros and the cons, virtual teaming does represent an option when various team members are located at different sites.

Even if the team you lead is not connected with groupware, do not underestimate the power of a simple conference call (particularly if a speakerphone is available) to allow the distant team member to be a part of the discussion.

Team Leader Technique: *Team meeting time can quickly flitter away if the team gets embroiled in philosophical discussions or focuses on minor issues which are more interesting or manageable than the problems they should be solving as a team. Creating a "parking lot" on a flip chart and posting it prominently in the room allows the team leader/facilitator to park items which may be good fodder for a future meeting, but not what the team needs to be discussing today. For the sake of trust, a wise leader keeps track of these items and includes opportunities for the team to address them in the future.*

Teams on Track

8

"Success is not a place at which one arrives but rather . . . the spirit with which one undertakes and continues the journey."[1]

Successful teams are driven by their purpose

The single most significant factor for a team is its purpose.

There are various groupings of people who may be called teams. The team label exists in both corporations and volunteer organizations. If the group of people has a vague, nonexistent, unclear, or low-priority purpose, then I would suggest they are not actually a team. They are teams only in the broadest sense of the word. Rather than quibble over nomenclature, or assume the role of team police, I would wish that people be aware they are simply not teams in a high-performance sense. Furthermore, they do not necessarily have the potential or need to be high-performance teams. For example:

- Co-workers in an office who meet to share information
- Members of an ongoing committee which is stipulated in the organizational bylaws
- A group which provides a functional service for the organization

If this sounds elitist or discriminating, then I take responsibility for my language and observation. It is only in cases when the individuals who are called a team identify something which they feel is compelling, which they must do, which no one else will do, which they can articulate, and which they are committed to work toward that a real team emerges.

There is nothing mysterious about a team which adopts a clear purpose and then moves toward that purpose with intentionality. It becomes a high-performance team when it delivers on its purpose. Its purpose is more than the sum of what the individuals on the team are doing. Its purpose is something which everyone on the team wants to help accomplish. Sometimes that purpose is accomplished and the team effort is concluded. Other times, the purpose is a broad, long-term objective on which the team works over a period of time.

Inside Team: *A new group of employees was hired and trained within my organization. The group was called the Customer Relations Team. Because this group joined the staff during the busiest season of our year, there was little time for the team leader to meet with the group as a team. The group learned the basics of their individual roles and then were turned loose to respond to customers all day long.*

A break in individual responsibilities allowed the new team to meet together and talk about what they could accomplish collectively. They adopted a reason for their existence (their purpose) and just as importantly, goals began to surface. They recognized they could contribute to the financial vitality of the whole organization by establishing sales goals. A friendly spirit of competition began to permeate their team meetings. They glimpsed that what they could do together was greater than handling customer responses and questions. They began to gel as a team.

A successful team is goal-focused

Recently I met with a group of new team leaders along with their teams. Earlier, I had provided training as they launched their teaming effort and crafted purpose statements. I also had the opportunity to be with them several times over a period of months. At this session, their executive asked me to remind them of my best wisdom, based on lessons I had learned, about team goal setting. I was to provide the springboard to enable the team leaders to lead their teams in goal setting.

With a narrow time frame—20 minutes—to deliver this "wisdom," I reminded them of eight truths about goals which experience tells me are foundational.

1. Don't obsess about goals. I had observed the tendency of staff in my organization (basically overachieving females) to spend lengthy sessions writing, editing, and tweaking goal statements. An unspoken assumption permeated their thinking that the "perfect goal" existed and they were determined to find it. And write it. And achieve it. When our executive set a deadline by which teams were expected to turn in their goals, there was loud wailing and a request for more time. She was adamant. We had to have our goals by the end of the month.

Looking back (as one of the ones who chafed at having to commit to goals so quickly in the team process), I recognize that if we hadn't been pushed, we might, 2 years later, still be polishing our initial set of goals.

2. Goals grow out of purpose. If the team's purpose statement is a clear direction or objective for the future, then goals should flow out of it naturally. Initial attempts at goal writing may result in lofty verbiage, actions lacking measurability, or goals unrelated to the purpose of the team.

Early efforts by teams in my organization turned out goals that were activity-based (rather than outcome-based). Innocuous statements like:

"Call all regional offices and offer assistance."
"Update policies, procedures, and guidelines."
"Create a buzz about an organization."
"Share information with each other."

were submitted as goals. We had lots of room to improve, and training was clearly indicated to move beyond these vague statements.

3. Remember, goals are best when thought of as part of the performance cycle. Setting goals is only the team's first step. The pursuit of the goal (What actions will be required to make the goal a reality? Who will do what? By when?) is the next identifiable action, followed by the evaluation of how we are doing. If the goal is to double sales of a product, the numbers are clear indicators of whether this is a realistic goal or not. Another element in the performance cycle is the monitoring of the goal. Measuring how well the team is doing necessitates picking the right yardstick and keeping up-to-date on goal progress. It may be the next element of the cycle, adjusting the goal, will need to occur. And then, the cycle begins all over again: set, pursue, evaluate, monitor, adjust, and begin again.

4. The best goals conform to the criteria of SMART (specific, measurable, achievable, relevant, timebound). This is more than a timeworn acronym. When the team applies SMART to its goals regularly, the team is able to tell whether it has accomplished what it set out to do. Specific, measurable, achievable, relevant, and timebound goals are goals which can be measured. The team will know whether it has succeeded or not.

The best goals are those which move beyond activity (such as "to provide 12 training sessions during the upcoming year") to an outcome-based goal ("to provide training sessions which will result in equipping leaders to begin 45 new organizations in our state by year-end").

5. Most goals are activities, pure and simple. Those who observe groups which are engaged in creating goals note the strong gravitational pull of activities.

Organizational culture is deeply immersed in activities. Individuals as well as teams who are people of action are looked to as good role models. At least they are doing something. Activities are not to be avoided or looked upon as lesser use of team time. But, activities should not be confused with goals. Activities are necessary because they lead to the accomplishment of a goal.

A team which wrestles with the question of what outcome will enable their purpose to become a reality is on the track toward team success.

6. The worst goals are those which are never set. Goals are the single means which enable a team to determine whether they are making progress on their stated purpose. Without taking the time to articulate goals, the team may continue to meet and discuss issues and share information. They may enjoy one another's company and socialize together. But at the end of a specified period of time, has the team accomplished anything? Probably not.

Without goals to which the team can link its success, the individual team members are likely to lose enthusiasm for any team meeting. After all, nothing happens as a result of their being together. Individuals continue to do individual tasks and work projects; but because the team has not set forth how they will look if they are successful (i.e., a measurable goal), the team is unfocused.

Goal setting for teams takes time and energy. It is, like many of the disciplines which impact teams, a process.

Teams get better at setting and performing their goals with time.

7. Having too many goals is the same as having no goals. Many teams are overly ambitious in their approach to setting goals. Although I don't know that there is a certain number of goals which a team should ideally set, I think the team intuition (or team collective IQ) would dictate that establishing goals in the double digits is likely to be counterproductive. Too many goals are difficult to track. If a team proudly declares it has 15 goals, the actions that are necessary to support that many goals would be lengthy.

One duo of team trainers note that "goal sludge" occurs when the team has multiple goals in place and tasks go uncompleted.[2] A better scenario is to focus on what is doable for the short term, say the next six months.

8. Goals are what we accomplish together that we couldn't do alone. Particularly with new teams, the tendency may be to list as team goals the activities which individuals on the team are charged with doing.

As tempting as that approach to goal setting may be, a wise team will avoid that habit. The team constantly asks itself, "Why do we exist?" (Their purpose.) And then, "How will we move toward accomplishing our purpose?" (What is it that the team can do collectively to make its purpose a reality? These actions translate into goals.)

An on-track team dares to measure its success

The team which is formed to accomplish a singular purpose (to enlist new leaders, to plan an event, to implement a training experience, to create a strategy, etc.) may find its goals consist of the very purpose for which the team was created.

As soon as the purpose is accomplished (the new leaders are enlisted, the event is planned, etc.) then the team ceases to function. That team measures its success by the ability to deliver what they came together to do.

Other teams, particularly in the workplace, live more in the realm of ongoing delivery of performance. Such is the case with the 21 teams within my organization. Each team has created its own purpose statement, but each must also wrestle with creating meaningful goals on an annual basis. Those goals are evaluated by an internal review group. The criteria used by the review group include:

- Is the goal an outcome-based goal rather than an activity?
- Is the goal measurable?
- Is the team's goal in sync with the corporate vision?
- Is the team's goal challenging when compared to other teams' goals?

Such review is appropriate in that each team will be rewarded with additional compensation if, and only if, the goal is achieved.

A goal is often measured by the application of one or more of a number of yardsticks including the most common:[3]

1. Speed/time: When the team surfaces a goal related to a process, the challenge becomes one of how quickly or how long it takes that process to occur.

2. Cost: Goals related to cost are quite common. How can the team deliver a product which is less expensive and therefore more attractive to customers?

Inside Team: *For a number of years, the production teams with a certain company had kept the costs of their product down to a very reasonable level. Each new product that the team was genuinely excited about was created amid a chorus of "Our customers will love this!" and "a must-have." The team frequently ordered large quantities of the item, thus ensuring the unit cost was low, and the cost to the customer was low. This practice was common until a new CFO questioned the large amounts of unsold product which had to be written off or reported during the annual audit. The teams became more cost conscious and driven to doing market research to determine products which would in fact sell to their audience.*

3. On-spec/expectations of quality: The criteria of on spec/expectations simply means "What does the customer expect?" Obviously customers expect error-free products, but they also expect products which are easy to use and ready on time, etc.

4. Positive yields: This category of measurement has been used as a catchall according to goal guru Douglas Smith.[4] Whereas the earlier metrics were objective, there is a subjective quality to this yardstick. For example, if a team wants to establish their company as the most respected brand of service or product, then the team will have to come to grips with how to measure respect in their line of business.

A successful team has an enabling leader

Team leaders come in a kaleidoscopic variety of shapes, sizes, temperaments, skill levels, experience, etc.

The fortunate team is one which early in its development grasps the understanding that their team leader is not their team boss. They do not, therefore, look to the team leader for all the ideas, to solve the problems of the team, to tell them what to do, to discipline wayward team members, to always be in charge, etc.

The team leader does not dodge the accountability of the role of leader. But, she is not caught up in the position or title of leader. She is willing to share leadership, to lead by example, and to let the purpose for which the team has been formed be the real boss of the team. She serves the team.

The best team leaders enable their teams to take on challenges. They are team members as well as leaders. And there is no one model for the best team leadership. There are multiple models, including these from my organization.

• Charlotte is a middle-aged information technology team leader whose team is primarily younger men whom she observes "could be my sons." She quickly acknowledges they trump her expertise in terms of certifications and technical credentials. She affirms the enthusiasm and innovation of her team who provides a wide spectrum of technology on a limited budget. She works alongside her team when the grunt work of moving work stations is the task of the day. Charlotte encourages both her team's creative solutions to internal challenges and their playfulness (such as sponsoring in-house contests to boost employee morale).

• Andrea, a leader of multiple teams, places a priority on injecting spontaneous fun into the hours of meetings which her teams must schedule. She juggles one team which includes a virtual team member. Constantly on the lookout for reasons to celebrate, her teams exude a spirit of fun. The leader's positive spirit is contagious among her team members who face stiff challenges such as staff vacancies and budget restrictions.

• Lynn leads a multifunctional team involving warehouse, mailroom, and duplication staff. Often found with his "hands on" some element of his team's work, Lynn is consistently upbeat. He is willing to pose performance challenges to his team and listen to their ideas for addressing the challenge. If the idea doesn't work, the team fails, not the team member who proposed it. A firm believer in cross-training, Lynn challenges his team to learn and try out a variety of functions.

• Linda leads the highly creative and independent team of graphic designers. They provide a broad scope of services ranging from ongoing magazine and book production to Web site design and many special projects such as stage or set designs. Linda perfected quick stand-up meetings in the early days of her team's life. She respects her team members' abilities and calls out their best. Known as a listener by her team, she assimilates input and leads the team to propose solutions to complex production issues. She is willing to be decisive after she gathers input from her team members and beyond.

Each of these team leaders shares a couple of common characteristics. They enable diverse groups of team members to focus on the contribution which the team can make. They put their egos on the back burner and nudge the team (or shove the team) toward what the team must do to succeed at accomplishing its goals. In addition, these leaders are not ideal models of what any other team leader needs to be. The characteristics they express and their style have developed in the context of the team with which they work. There may be a little of a chameleon-like quality to a good team leader. He or she assesses the makeup of the team, identifies what the performance challenges are, and leads in relationship to the team he or she has been dealt.

An on-track team gets better at process and task

Even a casual observer of team life notices the subtle balancing act which goes on as a team develops. The team makes strides toward accomplishing its goals. It identifies and pursues new goals, all in the cycle of performance. Simultaneously, an on-track team grows more skilled in the way it operates. I suspect many of the teams in my organization who sweated out the creation of purpose statements would be much more adept today, nearly 2 years into the teaming process, of producing a purpose statement. Are the team members any more brilliant, committed, or wise? No. They are just more accustomed to functioning as a team. They know whom to expect creativity from, who'll write on the whiteboard, who will wordsmith their effort, who will call time on their deliberations, etc.

The nuts and bolts of teaming are clearer to them as team members. The idiosyncrasies of fellow team members are better known. Team members are quicker to identify who is the most skilled on their team to implement a particular task. They have worked together in implementing projects over a period of time and have learned who is capable of what.

Inside Team: *In one organization, several members of a particular team had a history of being at odds with each other. The hallmarks of their team discussions were emotional outbursts, tension, and wounded feelings. There was a low level of cooperation for anything which the team might decide to do collaboratively. Scathing emails were not unusual between team members. Disagreement reigned. Each of the team members was a skilled, professional contributor; but the team, for whatever reasons, had never gelled. Outside of team meetings, members acknowledged something was wrong with the way they functioned. A neutral team member commented team meetings gave her a headache, but was clueless about how to bring about change.*

During a broad restructure, new team members were added to the original team. An outside leader was designated. Boundaries were established for the team by management (i.e., they had a clear mandate about expectations that team alone could fulfill). While the nucleus of the team never changed, the dynamics on the team began to shift. There seemed to be a willingness to place a moratorium on their previous team behavior. No mention was ever made of how the team operated previously. Operating guidelines were established and adhered to by the new team. They had a clean slate on which to write, and fortunately the team put their history of pettiness behind them and began to focus on what they could only accomplish together.

An on-track team is energized

How can you tell if a team is on track? The simplest way is to observe the team in its natural habitat—a meeting. An on-track team is engaged during the meeting. There is a spirit of "We're doing something which matters." There is a purpose which moves the meeting forward. Team members exude a sense of "I care about what we're deciding and here's my opinion." There's often a good-spirited give-and-take among team members, even when a team decision or solution brings about a polarity of opinion. The conflict is acknowledged and the team sets out to come to the best decision in spite of the conflict.

An energized team will frequently generate many more creative ideas which are goal-related. But the team is also aware that they must be disciplined, sorting through the ideas and evaluating the potential of each one in light of their goal. Unlike a team which "never met an idea it didn't like" and tried to implement every idea which came down the pike, an on-track team is able to discriminate. Through lively discussion, the best of the creative output rises to the top. The team gravitates toward the idea which from their collective IQ perspective is the best. That's the solution which is owned by the team and for which the team will work to make succeed.

Another approach of assessing whether a team is on track or not is to evaluate their results. Has the team been able to deliver on the goals which it established? If so, that's good evidence of a team which is on track. When it is obvious the team has failed to accomplish its goals, how does the team respond? An on-track team acknowledges it missed the mark. It takes success, and failure, as a team result. An on-track team resists playing the blame game by pointing to a fellow team member, another team, a process, or a technical glitch as the cause of their failure. "We messed up. We blew it. We may have set the wrong goal. What did we learn from this? We'll know better next time." These are the on-track team responses to failure.

Inside Team: *In my organization, one team which exists "to equip church and associational leaders to involve people in the mission of God"[5] is comprised of 7 very diverse, creative, and committed men and women. Their broad purpose statement opens the door for a variety of goals. Team meetings are punctuated with practical, and impossible, ideas which might turn church leaders into missions champions. Goals this team has pursued range from redesigning print pieces, to creating kits of new resources, to creating a Web site targeting a group of leaders, to a product with the unlikely name of* Missions for Dummies. *Partnerships with church planters, as well as with other teams in the building, are common fodder in this team's resolve to implement their purpose.*

Teams which have matured and mastered the foundational process skills such as communication, problem solving, decision making, etc., are headed for success. These teams do not waste valuable team time on insignificant issues. When tempted to digress from actions which will enable the team to meet their goals, a team member will surely suggest a particular issue be placed in the "parking lot" or discussed at some future date. There is an agreement among team members of what they must complete or do or agree upon for that day. This is an energized, on-track team.

Team Leader Technique: *To enable team members to understand each other and thus increase the likelihood they will succeed as a team, one team coach suggests a "Coat-of-Arms" exercise.[6] Each team member is given a flip chart sheet and set of colored markers and asked to design and draw a coat of arms that will enable other team members to know the important things about the individual. To get started, the leader might suggest the team include the most important accomplishment of their life, the single value from which they would never budge, and three words they'd like people to say about them at their funeral.*

Team
Breakdown

"Good people are good because they've come to wisdom through failure. We get very little wisdom from success, you know."[1]

Why teams get stuck

More often than not people come together to form a team with the best of intentions. The horizon is bright with possibilities. They care about the purpose of the group effort. They are willing to invest their time and energy to help the team purpose become a reality. Team members come to the table with diverse skills and gifts. The team is not unlike a vanload of passengers on a journey. What happens when inevitable obstacles appear on the road? Some teams will get stuck. They may be derailed, or stalled, or find themselves in a ditch. At the very least, they are jostled by the speed bumps.

What prompts a team to actually break down? This phenomenon is well known by experts who write about team dynamics and who call it "stuck teams."[2]

If you could eavesdrop on the conversations between members of a stuck team, you might hear comments like:

"What a waste of time."

"It's all show-and tell for the boss."

"There's nothing anyone can do."

"We have no clue as to what this all about."

"Nobody wants to talk about what's really going on."
"If this effort's so important, why don't they just give us more resources?"
"I knew this teamwork stuff was [just smoke and mirrors]."[3]

Why would team members voice such negative or disillusioned comments? Among many factors, at least these five are likely culprits:

Resistance to the concept of teaming
Unclear purpose
Poor team relationships
Lack of communication skill
Leadership skill gap

Resistance to the concept of teaming

The resistance factor is more likely to crop up in the workplace among staff teams than among volunteer teams. Possibly because employees are not often "consulted" about the decision to change structures, they therefore resist change. In other settings, where individuals may choose to become part of a team, resistance is not an issue.

Inside Team: *My organization, like many others, has a reputation for periodic reorganizations. A leadership change at the top level of leadership invariably brings about a shuffling of personnel and relationships. Savvy staff have learned to remain cool when titles, department configurations, even work stations, are changed. In our 2001 transition to teams, many long-time employees received the news about the changes with a wait-and-see attitude. Some team members were even heard to comment, "This team fad will pass. We'll be back to our old departments before long."*

There was no effort to sabotage the change; but there was little excitement, initially, about the idea of becoming teams.

In the midst of numerous internal moves and adjustments to new ways of working together, our top leader emphasized in more than one employee meeting, "This change is for the long term. You're not going to arrive at the office tomorrow and discover we have gone back to our former structure. Let's learn to be the best teams we can be!"

Two years into the transition to the team environment, some staff members are still waiting for the word that we are reverting to the old structure.

Individuals who have had little or no experience with working on teams are uncertain about what being a team means. Their past experiences in education and the workplace have been based on individual accomplishment. They were familiar with report cards, acquired degrees, and workplace rewards based on their personal efforts. If they had experience with teams, it was frequently tied to involvement in sports. Training can have a positive impact on resistance which is based on unfamiliarity with teams.

Inside Team: *One team leader encountered a mindset from her small, hardworking team: "Just tell us what you want us to do." As she tried to facilitate a session in which the team would surface goals for the future, the team members were frustrated. They were accustomed and very comfortable with the department structure. They were happy with their "boss." Their routine was being upset by suddenly being called upon to behave like a team.*

The team leader exercised patience with the staff as she interpreted to them what being a team might entail. Her task was made easier when her team grew with the addition of several newly hired members.

Now the old core group was, indeed, a new structure,
and the understandings of team were expanded.

Sometimes the resistance to being a team is
expressed by team members who hunker down into
their individual accountabilities or function. The atti-
tude of a team member who is willing to be responsi-
ble for his job, but not participate in team
collaboration, can be addressed by the team leader in
a one-on-one alignment discussion. As long as the
team leader is aware of the member's detachment (and
it is usually obvious to other team members as well),
the discussion can unfold. In this kind of conversa-
tion, the team leader seeks input from the team mem-
ber about why he or she appears to be unengaged with
the total direction of the team. Exploration about what
it would take for the team member to "buy in" to the
team purpose may also occur. It is possible some staff
do not choose to give the team effort a try.

Unclear purpose

A team usually develops a purpose statement in a couple of
different ways: either by receiving it from an outside entity
(management, mandate from another committee, etc.) or
by going through an exercise in which the team creates its
purpose statement.

In either case, the members of the team must have
their purpose in sharp focus. Their purpose answers the
question, Why do we exist? It is the one most important
thing about the team. If there is ambiguity or lack of clarity in the expression of that purpose, it is hardly surprising
the team would stumble.

My observation is that there is a certain amount of wig-
gle room between what the team calls its purpose statement and the next level of discussion which is What are
our goals? By this I mean if a team writes a purpose which
is directional and long-term like:

- To facilitate volunteer involvement in missions (Missions Involvement Team)
- To provide safeguards for protecting WMU assets, and to provide relevant, timely financial information (Accounting Team)
- To create and design products that serve as primary resources for people involved in missions, resulting in the growth of God's kingdom and financial contributions that enhance the work of WMU ministries (WMU Products Team)

then its goals must spell out the specifics by which they are trying to accomplish their purpose.

Obviously purpose statements like those in the examples are not measurable in and of themselves. The statement does establish a direction. The team may choose to keep its purpose statement in place indefinitely. However, the goals which grow out of the purpose statement are regularly changing, as the team achieves them.

If a team has settled on a purpose statement which is attainable in the short term, then upon completion of that purpose, the team thinks up a new purpose statement.

The only poor purpose statement is one which the team does not understand. Or, if they understand it, they deem it irrelevant. Since the team purpose is the property of the team, the team alone has the authority to revisit it, tweak it, and make any adjustments in the words.

A simple tool which a team can apply to its purpose statement consists of six criteria and ratings (see the following model):[4]

Team Purpose: _____

	Very low	Low	Average	High	Very High
Clarity				✓	
Relevance				✓	
Significance					✓
Believability		✓			
Urgency	✓				
Overall motivation			✓		

A discussion of this tool, after allowing team members to complete it, may lead to the strengthening of the team purpose. What would add urgency to our purpose? What makes our purpose statement low in believability?

Poor team relationships

An informal personality-type inventory tool to which I was introduced years ago categorizes everyone as either a

- Dolly Doer,
- Polly Practical,
- Lucy Logical, or
- Willa Watcher.

While the names are slightly comical, it is easy to see people fitting into at least one of these classifications, based on their personality style.

Life is a bit more complex, however, and team members who may act like Lucy Logical in one meeting have the habit of expressing a different side in the next meeting or maybe even in their next breath.

The common denominator of all teams is the unique men and women who comprise the team membership. I am convinced there is a limitless variety of people who may call your team home. There are those with quirky personalities. Others are winsome. Some team members would never choose to be a part of a group. Seated nearby is a nonstop talker. Some are dogmatic and know-it-all. Others seldom contribute unless directly questioned. There are team members who are pleasant and open, willing to take initiative. Others appear aloof and uninterested in what is going on in the team meeting. Some of the team members may have established friendships with others on their team. A few may be all business and "Let's get this meeting over!" Others are enthusiastic cheerleaders of any direction the group decides to take. Endless diversity.

The challenge is how do these unique individuals establish the working relationships to enable them to succeed as a team?

A foundational step is one which may be obvious: The team needs to recognize their differences. Growth in recognizing they are different occurs over the lifetime of the team as they work together. An understanding clicks in a team member's brain that others may see an issue differently than they do, and that viewing an issue differently is OK.

In an effort to create a culture in which differences are appreciated, a team leader may decide to introduce activities which lead the team to experience differences. For example, the simple True Colors activity involves using a bag of candy-coated chocolate candies. After each team member takes a handful of the candy, the leader asks each one to relate a work experience with the group. The kind of experience depends upon the color of candy which is most prominent in their hand: green—funniest work experience; blue—best work experience; red—most embarrassing work experience; yellow—most frightening work experience; and brown—most discouraging work experience.[5]

Another essential understanding about team member differences relates to the roles of the team members. Does everyone know the functional roles which the other team members have? That's a starting point. Additionally, team roles can be viewed through a variety of lenses. On the playing field of a meeting in which the team is involved, Glenn Parker, an observer and researcher of team behavior, identifies four types of team players:

1. Contributor: The task-oriented person who gets the team to focus on the short-term, specific issues facing the team.
2. Collaborator: The goal-directed member who sees the vision, mission, and strategic issues as paramount.
3. Communicator: The process-oriented person who works on the internal dynamics and interpersonal issues of the team.
4. Challenger: This person questions the goals, methods, and processes of the team and encourages the team to take well-conceived risks.[6]

Beyond understanding we're different and we have different roles, a basic tool which enables a diverse team to succeed is a shared understanding of how we will operate as a team as seen in the tangible creation of a set of team norms. Some teams even post these in their meeting room.

A successful team is often one which takes the time to focus on crafting a set of operating guidelines early in their time together as a team. The guidelines are the best thinking of the team as they anticipate how they would like to be treated in the teaming process and how they would be willing to interact with their co-team members. Thus operating guidelines often include statements which enable a team to become more cohesive and productive, while at the same time discourage behaviors which are counterproductive to team effectiveness.

Operating guidelines which will contribute to good team relationships include:

- Ask questions for clarification.
- Be on time for meetings.
- Actively listen to your teammates.
- Be open to new ideas.
- Be willing to go along with a consensus decision, even if you disagree with it.
- Don't promise anything you can't deliver.
- Be quick to share your knowledge, skills, and information.
- Follow through with any actions in timely and quality fashion.

If working relationships in a team setting are going to move forward, then all team members must be willing to be accountable to the guidelines, once they are established. And any team member can bring to the team's attention a breach in the guidelines.

There is one category of behavior which seldom adds to the team's effectiveness. In fact one writer calls them "blocking behaviors." Since team norms or guidelines are generally expressed in positive terms, these may not appear as guidelines but they are notable in that they will derail a team:

- Disagreeing without offering a rationale or alternatives
- Attacking other members of the team or in other ways being disrespectful
- Monopolizing a discussion or discouraging others from participating
- Excessive use of humor that diverts from the focus of the team
- Repetition of one's own ideas or refusing to let go of an issue that's been decided[7]

Lack of communication skill

An advertising executive once observed, "Today, communication itself is the problem. We have become the world's first overcommunicated society. Each year we send more and receive less."[8] The biggest assumption we may make is assuming communication has occurred.

Communication is a must between individuals, within families, in organizations, in the workplace, and certainly on teams. We cannot, not communicate. And what is our skill level? I believe teams which reach an impasse or self-diagnose themselves as stuck or stagnate may have a communication skill problem.

Inside Team: *In our company, employees are given opportunities to evaluate organizational morale by completing surveys. One of the areas which is consistently rated either very high or very low is that of communication. At one time I was frustrated and disappointed by the frequency with which employees rated internal communication as less than wonderful. In my mind, communication was a discipline you mastered. Then you delivered good communication, clearly and regularly. Today I am slightly more knowledgeable about communication and view it as a process, a complex process; a process at which a workforce and a team can grow more proficient, particularly if they identify that they are lagging in their skill set.*

A team is seldom criticized for communicating too much. A team may wade into murky waters when they do not communicate enough. The ripple effects of too little or lack of timely communication result in, to name a few, confusion, potential hard feelings, and wasted energy on the part of those outside the team.

Within teams, it is helpful to look at communication on two levels: those interactions between team members may be verbal or nonverbal. This is interpersonal communication. A second level of communication is the data, knowledge, facts, opinions, strategies, etc., of the team. This is informational communication and may occur between team members and with those outside the team as well.

Good communication enables a team to productively engage in those critical team processes of planning, problem solving, and decision making. Poor communication can create stagnation and cause bottlenecks to the team's effectiveness.

Among a variety of components of verbal communication, one stands out as particularly valuable: listening. At first glance listening may appear to be a low-level skill. Anybody can listen. Anyone can look like they are listening. Someone once noted, "Listening is more than waiting for your turn to talk." Many communication experts tout the value of active listening, a refined listening skill based on an interaction between team members. The spokesperson who proposes or interprets a path of action can be more clearly understood when other team members assume the position of active listener. The hallmarks of an active listener are comments such as:

- "I see."
- "Would you elaborate a little more?"
- "Go on."
- "In a nutshell then, you're saying . . ."
- "So you propose that we . . ."
- "If I'm hearing you correctly, then you are saying . . ."
- "You feel that . . ."
- "The team seems to agree on . . ."
- "The bottom line of this discussion is . . . "

Until the team sorts though the implications of one proposed solution or idea, it may be confusing to deal with substantively different ideas. Active listening can lead the team to explore thoroughly the idea currently on the table.

Team members sense they are, indeed, speaking the same language.

Leadership skill gap

There are as many models of team leadership as there are individuals who get tapped to lead teams. Nearly every leadership style has the potential for success, particularly when the leader has self-insight about what skills she needs help in. Successful team leaders keep the team focused on what the team has set out to do. The team purpose and team performance are the guiding stars, not the personality or position of the team leader.

Yet, there are individuals who end up in the team leader role who lack skills and are not overly conscious of what they lack. They are somewhat clueless. The team is on the verge of failure. The team itself can be a means by which that leader improves his or her skill and the fate of the team is salvaged.

Inside Team: *Because our organization transitioned from a functional department structure to a team-based culture, nearly all of the team leaders had been department directors or supervisors. A lot of discussion ensued in the early days of team formation about the skill set required to lead a team in contrast with supervising a department. Team leaders tried to be sensitive and refrain from "telling" the team what to do. They probably went overboard in holding back on making suggestions because they wanted to avoid giving the perception to team members "this is the boss talking."*

Over a period of months, the restraint which team leaders expressed in exercising authority began to pay off as lively exchanges occurred in team meetings. The team leader's suggestion was just one more opinion among the mix of opinions voiced by the team members.

There is an assortment of gaps or weak areas which observant team members may perceive in their leader. No lengthy hall-talk conversations need to occur between team members about the "problem" with the leader. Individual team members who feel an accountability to the team can step up at any time and enable the team to compensate for a deficit in its leader. Ineffectiveness on the part of the team leader does not necessarily spell disaster for the team, or mean the leader has to be replaced. A few areas in which the team may notice a deficit (and hopefully one leader would not display all of these deficits) and how the team can intervene:

• The team leader does not see the Big Picture or seem able to keep the team on target. Team members can be energetic catalysts for clarifying the mission of the team, its goals, and its approaches. During any meeting, a member can initiate a discussion with the team which compels the team to consider, "Where are we in terms of our purpose? What should we be doing next?"

• The team leader falters at building commitment and confidence among the team members. The individual team member who discerns the team spirit needs bolstering can assume the role of the team cheerleader. Offering constructive feedback about member contribution, affirmation for team member efforts, as well as leading the group to celebrate their success can galvanize a team.

• Lack of essential skills on the team goes unnoticed by the team leader. A savvy team member can point out to the team, "We seem to be missing (a functional or technical skill)." If the team concurs, then the problem the team must solve is how to appropriate the services of someone who can offer that skill. Suggesting a resource person join the team for a specific project is a worthy action from any team member.

- The team leader is slow or inept in managing relationships with people outside the team. A team depends upon its leader to take initiative for being the point of communication with outside people and even other teams. If the leader is lagging behind in this role and obstacles are looming on the horizon because of relationships with outsiders, a team member (or more than one) can assume responsibility for being the point person with outside entities. Of course the member would keep the team up-to-date about what he or she was doing.

- The team leader fails to equalize the plum assignments which the team implements. If the team leader either consciously or unconsciously hogs the majority of actions which the team members consider the plum assignments, a legitimate action of a team member is to bring up the subject of who is the best person to handle a certain assignment Some straight talk about equitable opportunities for all team members is appropriate.

- The team leader never seems to do any real work. Successful teams are led by individuals who are willing to serve the team. And in that service their names are just as likely to be listed as the person responsible when the work is grunt work. This particular habit of the team leader involves a sensitive delivery of the message. Thus, a team member may want to approach the team leader about it one-on-one. Once the team leader is aware the team has noticed his or her lack of work, the leader can respond.

Inside Team: *One leader who had a brief tenure in a company persisted in retreating to his office each day, closing the door, and maintaining a distance from his team. His demeanor of cheerfulness and professionalism when involved with his team in a meeting was not a substitute for availability and ongoing interaction among his team members. The small team was demor-*

alized by his detachment and ultimately complained, as a group, to the executive leadership. Ultimately his job ended because he did not master communication with his team.

Team Leader Technique: *To lead your team in improved communication, give each person a sheet of 8½-by-11 paper. Ask everyone to close his or her eyes and listen to your instructions, which are:*

Fold the sheet of paper I gave you in half. Fold it in half again. Tear off the right-hand corner. Turn the sheet over and tear off the left-hand corner.

After the team completes this activity, notice how different the results are. Lead the team in discussing why the results are different. Consider if the results would have been different if you had been able to open your eyes and see your own paper or the paper of your teammates. How would the results have been different if you had been able to ask questions? Would the results have been different if this was a team effort? How is this like or unlike the way we communicate as a team every day? To each other? To outsiders?

Conclusion

"Many attempts to communicate are nullified by saying too much."[1]

Well, reader, you are probably aware I have only begun to surface the wisdom, practical techniques, and potential which can be gained from team involvement. If you have found intriguing ideas which you are ready to apply as you lead a team or participate as a team member, or if you have resonated with one of my team learnings, then I have accomplished my purpose.

Your team involvement may be ongoing or infrequent. Your role varying from

- full-time team member or leader in the workplace, relating to multiple teams;
- volunteer leader or member of a church team or committee;
- leader or member of a community or educational team or board;
- participant in a shared-ministry team in a local church;
- member of an organizational or professional leadership team.

Here are a few things I am committed to practice as a result of my exploration and learning about teams. Perhaps one of these will be your resolution as well:

1. I want to be open to new insights about working with teams. When a team experience ends, reflect on why it was good, mediocre, or why it flopped. What one thing can you do in your next team experience to either ensure its success or prevent the team from falling into the same pothole you just endured?
2. I'll remember every team experience is unique. I know this is so because the purpose and people are different in each case. The chemistry of the team varies. Team dynamics defy reduction into a simple formula.
3. I will be an ongoing and intentional learner about teams. Do this by talking to other people who are involved in team efforts, reading, and applying things you haven't tried before.
4. I will anticipate being surprised when I am involved with a team. "Who would have ever thought that team could pull off . . .?"
5. I will grow in my skill as a team leader. No one ever arrives at the destination of omniscient team leader. But the next team I lead will benefit from those teams I have practiced on in the past.

Notes

Chapter 1
[1]Pat MacMillan, *The Performance Factor* (Nashville: Broadman & Holman Publishers, 2001), 30.
[2]Ibid., 31.

Chapter 2
[1]*The Columbia World of Quotations,* s.v. "Hubert H. Humphrey" [book online] (New York: Columbia University Press, 1996, accessed April 15, 2003); available from http://www.bartleby.com/66/50/29650.html; Internet.
[2]William Barclay, *A Spiritual Autobiography* (Grand Rapids, MI: William B. Eerdmans Publishing Company, 1975), 21.
[3]George Cladis, *Leading the Team-Based Church* (San Francisco: Jossey-Bass Publishers, 1999), 1.

Chapter 3
[1]Jon R. Katzenbach and Douglas K. Smith, *The Discipline of Teams* (New York: John Wiley & Sons, Inc., 2001), 138.
[2]Harriet B. Harral, "Gender Differences in Communication" (presentation at January Board Meeting of Woman's Missionary Union, Birmingham, AL, January 1996).
[3]Bobbi DePorter, *Quantum Learning* (New York: Dell Publishing, 1992), 125–26.
[4]Select, Assess & Train, "Communication," http://www.selectassesstrain.com/hint6.asp; Internet; accessed August 13, 2003.
[5]Pat MacMillan, *The Performance Factor* (Nashville: Broadman & Holman Publishers, 2001), 140ff.

Chapter 4
[1]Pat MacMillan, *The Performance Factor* (Nashville: Broadman & Holman Publishers, 2001), 44.
[2]This is the actual purpose statement for the Adult Resource Team at national WMU.
[3]MacMillan, *The Performance Factor,* 30.
[4]Jon R. Katzenbach and Douglas K. Smith, *The Wisdom of Teams* (Boston: Harvard Business School Press, 1993; reissue, New York: HarperPerennial, 1999), 91 (page citation is to reissue edition).
[5]MacMillan, *The Performance Factor,* 44ff.
[6]Mike Vance and Diane Deacon, *Think Out of the Box* (Franklin Lakes, NJ: Career Press, 1995), 85.
[7]Doug Hall, *Jump Start Your Brain* (New York: Warner Books, 1995), 245.

Chapter 5
[1]Lee Trevino, American professional golfer (available from http://tacomaweekly.tripod.com/Golf-Quotations.html; Internet; accessed June 17, 2003).
[2]Pat MacMillan, *The Performance Factor* (Nashville: Broadman & Holman Publishers, 2001), 123.
[3]Harvey Robbins and Michael Finley, *The New Why Teams Don't Work* (San Francisco: Berrett-Koehler Publishers, Inc., 2000), 35.
[4]Ibid., 40–41.
[5]*Combining Your Team's Ideas: Building Consensus Using Fist-to-Five* [articles online] (Olympia, WA: Freechild Project, 2003, accessed June 17, 2003); available from http://www.freechild.org/Firestarter/Fist2Five.htm; Internet.

Chapter 6
[1]James B. Simpson, comp., *Simpson's Contemporary Quotations*, s.v. "Hans Magnus Enzensberger" (as quoted by Hans Haacke) [book online] (Boston: Houghton Mifflin Company, 1988, accessed July 10, 2003); available from http://www.bartleby.com/63/61/5861.html; Internet.
[2]Harvey Robbins and Michael Finley, *The New Why Teams Don't Work* (San Francisco: Berrett-Koehler Publishers, Inc., 2000), 76–89.
[3]Bradford Glaser, *Black Bear: A Team Adventure* (King of Prussia, PA: HRDQ, 1993, 1994). Web site: www.hrdq.com.
[4]Pat MacMillan, *The Performance Factor* (Nashville: Broadman & Holman Publishers, 2001), 143–49.

Chapter 7
[1]James B. Simpson, comp., *Simpson's Contemporary Quotations,* s.v. "Barry Bingham Jr." [book online] (Boston: Houghton Mifflin Company, 1988, accessed May 8, 2003); available from http://www.bartleby.com/63/97/2097.html; Internet.
[2]Pat MacMillan, *The Performance Factor* (Nashville: Broadman & Holman Publishers, 2001), 262.
[3]Kerry Patterson et al., *Crucial Conversations* (New York: McGraw-Hill, 2002), 164–65.
[4]Glenn Parker, *Team Depot: A Warehouse of Over 585 Tools to Reassess, Rejuvenate, and Rehabilitate Your Team* (San Francisco: Jossey-Bass/Pfeiffer, 2002), 345.
[5]Jon R. Katzenbach and Douglas K. Smith, *The Discipline of Teams* (New York: John Wiley & Sons, Inc., 2001), 151–77.

Chapter 8

[1]James B. Simpson, comp., *Simpson's Contemporary Quotations,* s.v. "Alex Noble" [book online] (Boston: Houghton Mifflin Company, 1988, accessed May 9, 2003); available from http://www.bartleby.com/63/53/5253.html; Internet.

[2]Harvey Robbins and Michael Finley, *The New Why Teams Don't Work* (San Francisco: Berrett-Koehler Publishers, Inc., 2000), 41.

[3]Douglas K. Smith, *Make Success Measurable!* (New York: John Wiley & Sons, Inc., 1999), 30–40.

[4]Ibid., 38.

[5]This is the actual purpose statement of the Churchwide Resource Team at national WMU.

[6]Pat MacMillan, *The Performance Factor* (Nashville: Broadman & Holman Publishers, 2001), 144.

Chapter 9

[1]James B. Simpson, comp., *Simpson's Contemporary Quotations,* s.v. "William Saroyan" [book online] (Boston: Houghton Mifflin Company, 1988, accessed May 9, 2003); available from http://www.bartleby.com/63/20/5320.html; Internet.

[2]Jon R. Katzenbach and Douglas K. Smith, *The Wisdom of Teams* (Boston: Harvard Business School Press, 1993; reissue, New York: HarperPerennial, 1999), 149ff. (page citation is to reissue edition).

[3]Ibid., 151.

[4]Pat MacMillan, *The Performance Factor* (Nashville: Broadman & Holman Publishers, 2001), 53.

[5]*Brain Training for Teams* (Salt Lake City: Franklin Covey Company, 2000); card pack.

[6]Glenn Parker, *Team Depot: A Warehouse of Over 585 Tools to Reassess, Rejuvenate, and Rehabilitate Your Team* (San Francisco: Jossey-Bass/Pfeiffer, 2002), 142.

[7]Ibid., 163.

[8]James B. Simpson, comp., *Simpson's Contemporary Quotations,* s.v. "Al Ries" [book online] (Boston: Houghton Mifflin Company, 1988, accessed May 8, 2003); available from http://www.bartleby.com/63/21/2221.html; Internet.

Conclusion

[1]James B. Simpson, comp., *Simpson's Contemporary Quotations,* s.v. "Robert Greenleaf" [book online] (Boston: Houghton Mifflin Company, 1988, accessed May 15, 2003); available from http://www.bartleby.com/63/55/2155.html; Internet.

Bibliography

Barclay, William. *A Spiritual Autobiography.* Grand Rapids, MI: William B. Eerdmans Publishing Company, 1975.

Brain Training for Teams (card pack). Salt Lake City: Franklin Covey Company, 2000).

Cladis, George. *Leading the Team-Based Church.* San Francisco: Jossey-Bass Publishers, 1999.

DePorter, Bobbi. *Quantum Learning: Unleashing the Genius in You.* New York: Dell Publishing, 1992.

Hall, Doug. *Jump Start Your Brain.* New York: Warner Books, 1995.

Harrington-Mackin, Deborah. *The Team Building Tool Kit.* New York: American Management Association, 1994.

Heller, Robert. *Managing Teams.* New York: DK Publishing Merchandise, 1999.

Katzenbach, Jon R., and Douglas K. Smith. *The Wisdom of Teams.* Boston: Harvard Business School Press, 1993; reissue, New York: HarperPerennial, 1999.

_____. *The Discipline of Teams.* New York: John Wiley & Sons, Inc., 2001.

Lencioni, Patrick. *The Five Dysfunctions of a Team.* San Francisco: Jossey-Bass Publishers, 2002.

Lipman-Blumen, Jean, and Harold J. Leavitt. *Hot Groups.* New York: Oxford University Press, 2001.

MacMillan, Pat. *The Performance Factor.* Nashville: Broadman & Holman Publishers, 2001.

Maxwell, John C. *The 17 Indisputable Laws of Teamwork.* Nashville: Thomas Nelson Publishers, 2001.

Parker, Glenn. *Team Depot: A Warehouse of Over 585 Tools to Reassess, Rejuvenate, and Rehabilitate Your Team.* San Francisco: Jossey-Bass/Pfeiffer, 2002.

_____. *Team Players and Teamwork.* San Francisco: Jossey-Bass Publishers, 1996.

Patterson, Kerry, Joseph Grenny, Ron McMillan, and Al Switzler. *Crucial Conversations: Tools for Talking When Stakes Are High.* New York: McGraw-Hill, 2002.

Robbins, Harvey, and Michael Finley. *The New Why Teams Don't Work.* San Francisco: Berrett-Koehler Publishers, 2000.

Smith, Douglas K. *Make Success Measurable!* New York: John Wiley & Sons, Inc., 1999.

Vance, Mike, and Diane Deacon. *Think Out of the Box.* Franklin Lakes, NJ: Career Press, 1995.